Acoustic 70s Playlist

FABER ƒƒ MUSIC

© 2005 by International Music Publications Ltd
First published by International Music Publications Ltd in 2005
International Music Publications Ltd is a Faber Music company
3 Queen Square, London WC1N 3AU

Music arranged and engraved by Artemis Music Ltd.
(www.artemismusic.com)
Printed in England by Caligraving Ltd
All rights reserved

ISBN 0-571-52499-0

To buy Faber Music publications
or to find out about the full range of titles available,
please contact your local music retailer
or Faber Music sales enquiries:

Faber Music Ltd, Burnt Mill, Elizabeth Way, Harlow, CM20 2HX England
Tel: +44(0)1279 82 89 82
Fax: +44(0)1279 82 89 83
sales@fabermusic.com
fabermusic.com

How to use this book

All the songs in this book have been carefully arranged to sound great on the acoustic guitar. They are in the same keys as the original recordings, and where possible authentic chord voicings have been used, except where an alternative voicing more accurately reflects the overall tonality.

Where a capo was used on the original track, it is indicated at the top of the song under the chord boxes. If you don't have a capo, you can still play the song, but it won't sound in the same key as the original. Where a song is played in an altered tuning, that is also indicated at the top of the song.

Understanding chord boxes

Chord boxes show the neck of your guitar as if viewed head on – the vertical lines represent the strings (low E to high E, from left to right), and the horizontal lines represent the frets.

An x above a string means 'don't play this string'.

A o above a string means 'play this open string'.

The black dots show you where to put your fingers.

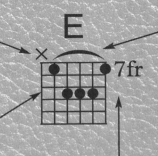

A curved line joining two dots on the fretboard represents a 'barre'. This means that you flatten one of your fretting fingers (usually the first) so that you hold down all the strings between the two dots, at the fret marked.

A fret marking at the side of the chord box shows you where chords that are played higher up the neck are located.

Tuning your guitar

The best way to tune your guitar is to use an electronic tuner. Alternatively, you can use relative tuning – this will ensure that your guitar is in tune with itself, but won't guarantee that you will be in tune with the original track (or any other musicians).

How to use relative tuning

Fret the low E string at the 5th fret and pluck – compare this with the sound of the open A string. The two notes should be in tune – if not, adjust the tuning of the A string until the two notes match.

E A D G B E

Tune A string to this note

Repeat this process for the other strings according to this diagram:
Note that the B string should match the note at the 4th fret of the G string, whereas all the other strings match the note at the 5th fret of the string below.

As a final check, ensure that the bottom E string and top E string are in tune with each other.

Contents

Ain't No Sunshine

Words and Music by
BILL WITHERS

Am⁷   Em⁷   G⁷   Em⁷*   Dm⁷*   Am⁹

♩ = 73

Verse 1   4/4 | N.C. | Am⁷   Em⁷ G⁷
Ain't no sunshine when she's   gone,
| Am⁷ | Em⁷ G⁷
It's not warm when she's away.
| Am⁷ | Em⁷*
Ain't no sunshine when she's go - one
                                | Dm⁷*
And she's always gone too long
                    | Am⁷   Em⁷ G⁷
Anytime she goes away.

Verse 2 | Am⁷ | Em⁷ G⁷
Wonder this time where she's gone?
| Am⁷ | Em⁷ G⁷
Wonder if she's gone to stay?
| Am⁷ | Em⁷*
Ain't no sunshine when she's go - one
                                | Dm⁷*
And this house just ain't no home
                    | Am⁷   Em⁷ G⁷
Anytime she goes away.

Bridge | Am⁷

> And I know, I know, I know, I know,

‖: N.C.   x4
                                          :‖

> I know, I know, I know, I know,

> I know, I know, I know, I know, I know,

| |

> I   know, hey, I ought to leave the young thing alone,

| Am⁷   Em⁷ G⁷

> But ain't no sunshine when she's   gone._____

Verse 3 | Am⁷   Em⁷ G⁷

> Ain't no sunshine when she's   gone,

| Am⁷ | Em⁷ G⁷

> Only darkness every day.

| Am⁷ | Em⁷*

> Ain't no sunshine when she's go - one

                                 | Dm⁷*

> And this house just ain't no home

                        | Am⁷   Em⁷ G⁷

> Anytime she goes away.

| Am⁷ | Em⁷ G⁷

> Anytime she goes away.

| Am⁷ | Em⁷ G⁷

> Anytime she goes away.

| Am⁷ | Em⁷ G⁷ | Am⁹   ‖

> Anytime she goes away.

(Is This The Way To) Amarillo?

Words and Music by
NEIL SEDAKA AND HOWARD GREENFIELD

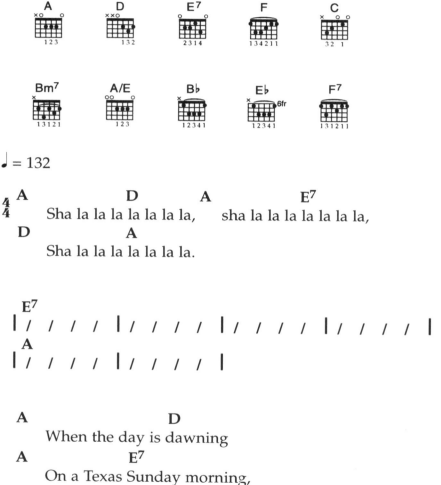

♩ = 132

Intro

4/4

A   D   A   E⁷
Sha la la la la la la la,   sha la la la la la la la,

D   A
Sha la la la la la la la.

Link

E⁷
| / / / / / | / / / / / | / / / / / | / / / / / |

A
| / / / / / | / / / / / |

Verse 1

A   D
When the day is dawning

A   E⁷
On a Texas Sunday morning,

A   D
How I long to be there

A   E⁷
With Marie who's waiting for me there.

F   C   F   C
Every lonely city   where I hang my hat

F   C   Bm⁷   E⁷
Ain't as half as pretty   as where my baby's at.

Chorus

A   D
Is this the way to Amarillo?

A   E⁷
Every night I've been hugging my pillow

A   D
Dreaming dreams of Amarillo

A/E   E⁷ A
And sweet Marie who waits for me.

          D
Show me the way to Amarillo

A   E⁷
I've been weeping like a willow

A   D
Crying over Amarillo

A/E   E⁷ A
And sweet Marie who waits for me.

Link 2

A   D   A   E⁷
Sha la la la la la la la, sha la la la la la la la,

D   A
Sha la la la la la la la.

E⁷   A
And Marie who waits for me.

Verse 2

A   D
There's a church bell ringing

A   E⁷
With a song of joy that it's singing

A   D
For the sweet Maria

A   E⁷
And the guy who's coming to see her.

F   C   F   C
Just beyond the highway there's an open plain

F   C   Bm⁷   E⁷
And it keeps me going through the wind and rain.

Chorus 2

A   D
Is this the way to Amarillo?
A   E⁷
Every night I've been hugging my pillow
A   D
Dreaming dreams of Amarillo
A/E   E⁷   A
And sweet Marie who waits for me.
                      D
Show me the way to Amarillo
A   E⁷
I've been weeping like a willow
A   D
Crying over Amarillo
A/E   E⁷   A
And sweet Marie who waits for me.

Link 3

A   D   A   E⁷
Sha la la la la la la la,   sha la la la la la la la,
D   A
Sha la la la la la la la.
E⁷   A
And Marie who waits for me.

Link 4

‖: B♭   E♭   B♭   F⁷
Sha la la la la la la la,   sha la la la la la la la,
E♭   B♭
Sha la la la la la la la.
F⁷   B♭
And Marie who waits for me. :‖ *repeat to fade*

10

All The Young Dudes

Words and Music by
DAVID BOWIE

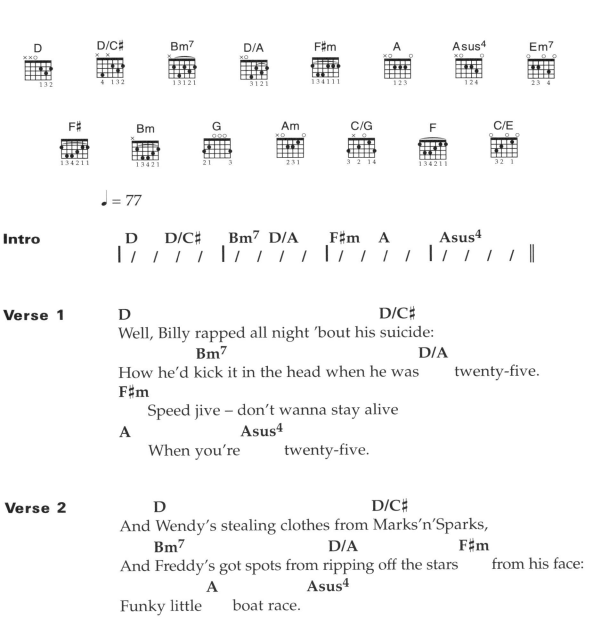

♩ = 77

Intro

D   D/C♯   Bm⁷ D/A   F♯m   A   Asus⁴

| / / / / | / / / / | / / / / | / / / / ‖

Verse 1

   D   D/C♯
Well, Billy rapped all night 'bout his suicide:
      Bm⁷   D/A
How he'd kick it in the head when he was   twenty-five.
F♯m
     Speed jive – don't wanna stay alive
A   Asus⁴
   When you're   twenty-five.

Verse 2

      D   D/C♯
And Wendy's stealing clothes from Marks'n'Sparks,
    Bm⁷   D/A   F♯m
And Freddy's got spots from ripping off the stars   from his face:
             A   Asus⁴
Funky little   boat race.

Prechorus

Em⁷
The television man is crazy,
    F♯   Bm
Saying we're juvenile delinquent wrecks.
   G   D   A   Asus⁴
Oh man, I need T.V. when I got T. Rex._____

Oh brother, you guessed – I'm a dude, dad.

Chorus

D D/C♯   Bm⁷
 All the young dudes____ (hey, dudes!)
D/A   Am
Carry the news.____ (where are ya?)
C/G   F   C/E   G C A
Boogaloo dudes____ (stand up, c'mon!) carry the news.____
D D/C♯   Bm⁷
 All the young dudes____ (I wanna hear you)
D/A   Am
Carry the news.____ (I wanna see you)
C/G   F
Boogaloo dudes____ (and I want to talk to you)
C/E   G C   A
Carry the news.___
(All of you…   now).

Verse 3

   D   D/C♯
Now Jimmy's looking sweet 'cause he dresses like a queen,
    Bm⁷   D/A
But he can kick like a mule – it's a real mean team –
F♯m   A   Asus⁴
 But we can love, oh yes, we can love.

Verse 4

    D   D/C♯
And my brother's back at home with his Beatles and his Stones,
   Bm⁷   D/A
We never got it off on that revolution stuff:
F♯m   A   Asus⁴
 What a drag – too many snags.

Prechorus 2

            Em⁷
Well, I've drunk a lot of wine and I'm feeling fine,
     F♯   Bm
Gonna race some cat to bed.
Bm⁷ G   D
Oh, is there concrete all around
             A   Asus⁴
Or is it in my   head?_____   Yeah, I'm a dude, yeah.

Chorus 2

𝄆 D D/C♯   Bm⁷
    All the young dudes____ (hey, dudes!)
D/A   Am
Carry the news.____ (where are ya?)
C/G   F   C/E   G   C   A
Boogaloo dudes____ (stand up!) carry the news.____
D D/C♯   Bm⁷
    All the young dudes____ (I wanna hear ya)
D/A   Am
Carry the news.____ (I wanna see you)
C/G   F
Boogaloo dudes____ (and I want to relate to you)
C/E   G   C   A
Carry the news.___   𝄇 *repeat Chorus to fade, vocal ad lib.*

American Woman

Words and Music by
RANDY BACHMAN, BURTON CUMMINGS,
JIM KALE AND GARRY PETERSON

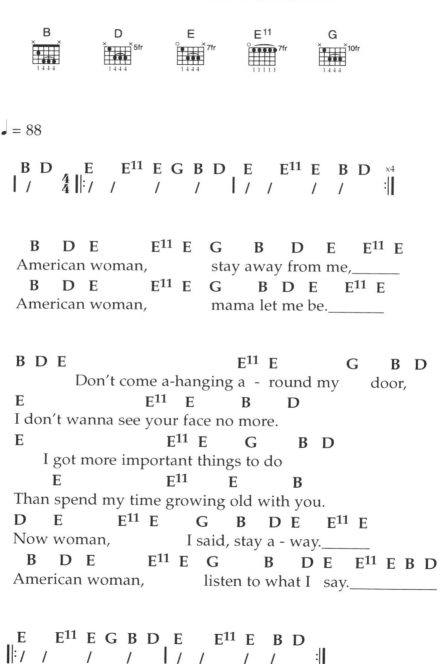

♩ = 88

Intro

B D   E   E¹¹ E G B D   E   E¹¹ E   B D   x4

Chorus

B   D   E   E¹¹ E G   B   D   E   E¹¹ E
American woman,   stay away from me,_____
B   D   E   E¹¹ E G   B D E   E¹¹ E
American woman,   mama let me be._____

Verse 1

B D E   E¹¹ E   G   B D
Don't come a-hanging a - round my   door,
E   E¹¹ E   B   D
I don't wanna see your face no more.
E   E¹¹ E   G   B D
I got more important things to do
E   E¹¹   E   B
Than spend my time growing old with you.
D   E   E¹¹ E   G   B   D E   E¹¹ E
Now woman,   I said, stay a - way._____
B   D E   E¹¹ E G   B   D E   E¹¹ E B D
American woman,   listen to what I   say._____

Link

E   E¹¹ E G B D E   E¹¹ E   B D

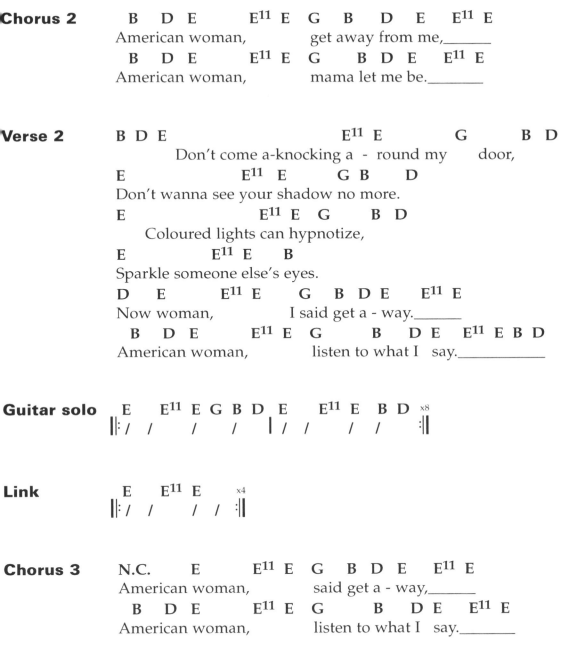

Chorus 2

  B D E   E¹¹ E G B   D E   E¹¹ E
American woman,   get away from me,_____
  B D E   E¹¹ E G   B D E   E¹¹ E
American woman,   mama let me be._____

Verse 2

  B D E   E¹¹ E   G   B D
     Don't come a-knocking a - round my   door,
E   E¹¹ E   G B   D
Don't wanna see your shadow no more.
E   E¹¹ E G   B D
   Coloured lights can hypnotize,
E   E¹¹ E   B
Sparkle someone else's eyes.
D   E   E¹¹ E   G B D E   E¹¹ E
Now woman,   I said get a - way._____
  B D E   E¹¹ E G   B   D E E¹¹ E B D
American woman,   listen to what I say._____

Guitar solo

E   E¹¹ E G B D E   E¹¹ E B D ^{x8}

Link

E   E¹¹ E   ^{x4}

Chorus 3

N.C.   E   E¹¹ E G B D E   E¹¹ E
American woman,   said get a - way,_____
  B D E   E¹¹ E G   B   D E   E¹¹ E
American woman,   listen to what I say._____

Verse 3

B D E E^{11} E   G   B D
Don't come a-hanging a - round my   door,

E E^{11} E   G B   D
Don't wanna see your face no more.

E E^{11} E   G   B   D
I don't need your war machines,

E E^{11} E   B D
I don't need your ghetto scenes.

E E^{11} E G   B D
Coloured lights can hypnotize,

E E^{11} E G B
Sparkle someone else's eyes.

D   E E^{11} E   G   B   D   E E^{11} E
Now woman,   get away from me._____

 B   D E E^{11} E   B D E E^{11} E
American woman,   mama, let me be._____

Coda

B D E E^{11} E   B   D   E
   Go, gotta   get away, gotta get away now go, go, go.

B   D   E   B D   E
   I'm gonna leave you, woman,   gonna leave you woman.

B   D   E E^{11} E B D   E E^{11} E
   Bye-bye,   bye-bye,_____

B   D   E E^{11} E B D   E E^{11} E
   Bye-bye,   bye-bye._____

B D   E E^{11} E B D E E^{11} E   B D
   You're no good for   me,   I'm no good for   you.

E E^{11} E   B D
Gonna look you right in the eye,

E E^{11} E
Tell you what I'm gonna   do:

   B   D   E E^{11} E   B   D   E E^{11} E
You know I'm gonna leave,   you know I'm gonna go,_____

   B   D   E E^{11} E
You know I'm gonna leave,

    B   D   E E^{11} E   B   D   E
You know I'm gonna go,   woman,   I'm gonna leave…

(fade)

16

Andy Warhol

Words and Music by
DAVID BOWIE

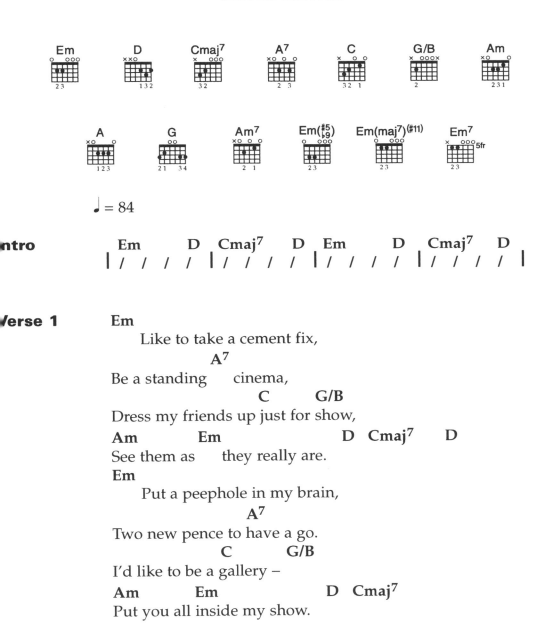

$\downarrow$ = 84

Intro

Em	D	Cmaj7	D	Em	D	Cmaj7	D

Verse 1

Em
Like to take a cement fix,
      A7
Be a standing   cinema,
           C   G/B
Dress my friends up just for show,
Am   Em   D   Cmaj7   D
See them as   they really are.
Em
Put a peephole in my brain,
          A7
Two new pence to have a go.
           C   G/B
I'd like to be a gallery –
Am   Em   D   Cmaj7
Put you all inside my show.

Chorus

```
D    A     Em    C
Andy Warhol looks a scream,
A        C    G    C
Hang him on my wall.
D    A     Em   C
Andy Warhol, silver screen –
        A        C    G   Am⁷  A
Can't tell them apart at all._____
```

Chorus

D   A   Em   C
Andy Warhol looks a scream,
A   C   G   C
Hang him on my wall.
D   A   Em   C
Andy Warhol, silver screen –
        A   C   G Am^7 A
Can't tell them apart at all._____

Link

Em   D $Cmaj^7$ D   Em   D $Cmaj^7$ D
| / / / / / | / / / / / | / / / / / | / / / / |

Verse 2

Em
    Andy walking, Andy tired,
                A^7
Andy take a little   snooze.
                    C   G/B
Tie him up when he's fast asleep,
Am   Em   D $Cmaj^7$ D
Send him on a pleasant cruise.
Em
      When he wakes up on the sea,
                        A^7
He's sure to think of me and you;
                        C   G/B
He'll think about paint and he'll think about glue –
        Am   Em   D $Cmaj^7$
What a jolly boring thing to do.

Chorus 2

D   A   Em   C
Andy Warhol looks a scream,
A   C   G   C
Hang him on my wall.
D   A   Em   C
Andy Warhol, silver screen –
        A   C   G Am^7 A
Can't tell them apart at all._____

Chorus 3   D   A   Em   C

Andy Warhol looks a scream,

A   C   G   C

Hang him on my wall.

D   A   Em   C

Andy Warhol, silver screen –

        A   C   G   Am^7 A

Can't tell them apart at all._____

Coda

Em   Em($^{\sharp 5}_{\flat 9}$)

| / / / / | / / / / | / / / / | / / / / |

Em(maj^7)($^{\sharp 11}$) Em($^{\sharp 5}_{\flat 9}$)   Em(maj^7)($^{\sharp 11}$)

| / / / / | / / / / |

Em($^{\sharp 5}_{\flat 9}$)   Em(maj^7)($^{\sharp 11}$) Em^7

| / / / / | / / / / | / / / / |

Em($^{\sharp 5}_{\flat 9}$)   Em(maj^7)($^{\sharp 11}$)

| / / / / | / / / / | / / / / | / / / / |

Em

| / / / / | / / / / | / / / / | / ‖

Box Of Rain

Words and Music by
ROBERT HUNTER AND PHIL LESH

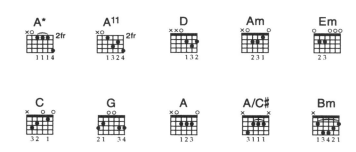

♩ = 112

Intro

Verse 1

D   Am
  Look out of any window
Em   C   G
Any morning, any evening, any day.
D   Am   Em
  Maybe the sun is shining, birds are winging,
  G   A
No rain is falling from a heavy sky.

Chorus

D   G
  What do you want me to do,
  Am   Em   D
To do for you to see you through?
      C   D
For this is all a dream we dreamed
     Am   G
One afternoon, long ago.

Verse 2

```
D                Am          Em
   Walk out of any doorway, feel your way,
C                              G
Feel your way like the day before.
D              Am
   Maybe you'll find direction,
  Em                         G              A
Around some corner where it's been waiting to meet you.
```

Chorus 2

```
D                G
   What do you want me to do,
  Am                         Em   D
To watch for you while you are sleep - ing?
     Am              C
Then please don't be surprised
           G              D
When you find me dreaming     too.
```

Guitar solo

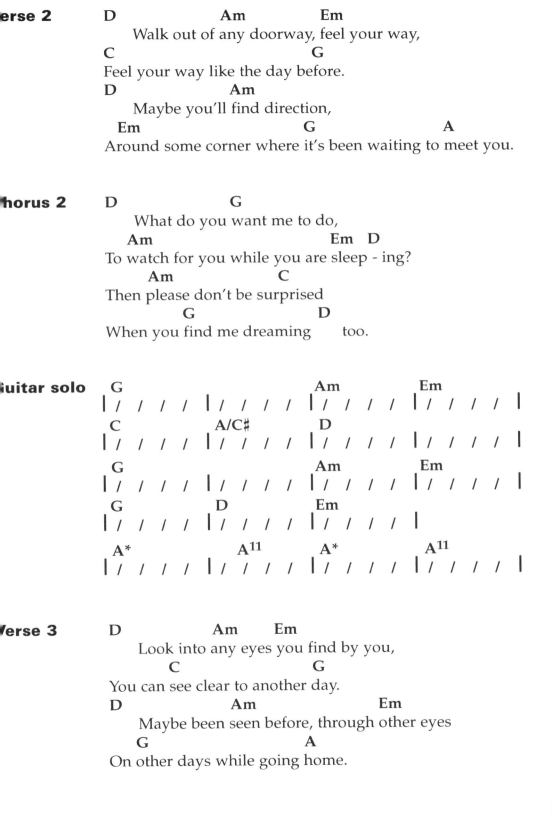

Verse 3

```
D              Am      Em
   Look into any eyes you find by you,
       C                 G
You can see clear to another day.
D              Am              Em
   Maybe been seen before, through other eyes
   G                      A
On other days while going home.
```

Chorus 3

D   G
What do you want me to do,
  Am   Em   D
To do for you to see you through?
    C   Em
It's all a dream we dreamed
        D   G
One afternoon, long ago.

Verse 4

D   Am
Walk into splintered sunlight,
Em   C   G
Inch your way through dead dreams to another land.
D   Am
Maybe you're tired and broken,
    Em   G
Your tongue is twisted with words half spoken
    A
And thoughts unclear.

Chorus 4

D   G
What do you want me to do,
  Am   Em   D
To do for you to see you through?
  Am   C
A box of rain will ease the pain,
    G   D
And love will see you through.

G   Am   Em
    Just a box of rain, wind and water,
  C   A
Believe it if you need it,
       D
If you don't just pass it on.
G   Am   Em
    Sun and shower, wind and rain,
G   D
In and out the window
    Em   A
Like a moth before a flame.

         D   Em
And it's just a box of rain,
      G   D
I don't know who put it there,
           Bm
Believe it if you need it,
  G   A
Or leave it if you dare.

        D   Em
And it's   just a box of rain,
     G   D
Or a ribbon for your hair;
        Em
Such a long, long time to be gone,
    G   D   C G D A
And a short time to be there._____ ‖

Brain Damage/Eclipse

Words and Music by
GEORGE ROGER WATERS

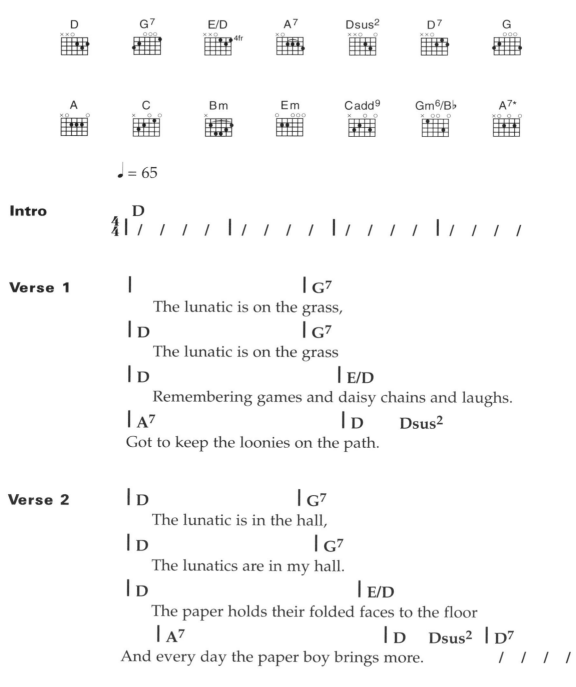

♩ = 65

Intro

| D
4/4 | / / / / | / / / / | / / / / | / / / /

Verse 1

| | G⁷
  The lunatic is on the grass,
| D | G⁷
  The lunatic is on the grass
| D | E/D
  Remembering games and daisy chains and laughs.
| A⁷ | D   Dsus²
Got to keep the loonies on the path.

Verse 2

| D | G⁷
  The lunatic is in the hall,
| D | G⁷
  The lunatics are in my hall.
| D | E/D
  The paper holds their folded faces to the floor
| A⁷ | D   Dsus² | D⁷
And every day the paper boy brings more.   / / / /

Chorus

|G |A
And if the dam breaks open many years too soon
      |C |G
And if there is no room upon the hill
| |A
And if your head explodes with dark forebodings too
      |C |G   Bm |Em   A
I'll see you on the dark side of the moon.   / / / /

Verse 3

|D |G^7
The lunatic is in my head,
|D |G^7
The lunatic is in my head.
|D |E/D
You raise the blade,   you make the change;
|A^7 |D   Dsus^2
You re-arrange me 'til I'm sane.
|D
You lock the door
    |E/D
And throw away the key.
      |A^7 |D   Dsus^2 |D^7
There's someone in my head but it's not me.

Chorus 2

|G |A
And if the cloud bursts, thunder in your ear
      |C |G
You shout and no-one seems to hear.
| |A
And if the band you're in starts playing different tunes
      |C |G   Bm |Em   A
I'll see you on the dark side of the moon.   / / / /

Coda

segue into **ECLIPSE**

$\quad$ ♩. = 45

Intro

$\begin{smallmatrix}6\\8\end{smallmatrix}$ | D $\qquad$ Cadd⁹ $\qquad$ Gm⁶/B♭ $\qquad$ A⁷*

$\begin{smallmatrix}6\\8\end{smallmatrix}$| / / / / / / | / / / / / / | / / / / / / | / / / / / /

Verse

| D
All that you touch
$\qquad$| Cadd⁹
And all that you see
$\qquad$| Gm⁶/B♭
And all that you taste,
| A⁷*
$\qquad$ All you feel,
$\qquad$| D
And all that you love
$\qquad$| Cadd⁹
And all that you hate
| Gm⁶/B♭
All you distrust
| A⁷*
$\qquad$ All you save
$\qquad$| D
And all that you give
$\qquad$| Cadd⁹
And all that you deal
$\qquad$| Gm⁶/B♭
And all that you buy,

  | A⁷*
Beg, borrow or steal,

  | D
And all you create

   | Cadd⁹
And all you destroy

   | Gm⁶/B♭
And all that you do

    | A⁷*
And all that you say

   | D
And all that you eat,

   | Cadd⁹
And everyone you meet

    | Gm⁶/B♭
And all that you slight,

   | A⁷*
And everyone you fight

   | D
And all that is now

    | Cadd⁹
And all that is gone

   | Gm⁶/B♭
And all that's to come

   | A⁷* | D
And everything under the sun is in tune

       | Cadd⁹ | Gm⁶/B♭ | D   ‖
But the sun is eclipsed by the moon._____

Bright Eyes

Words and Music by
MIKE BATT

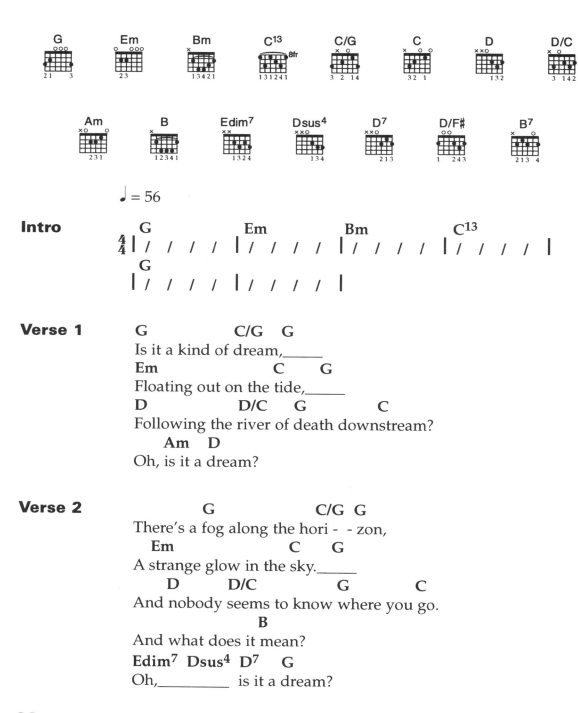

$\downarrow$ = 56

Intro

           G   Em   Bm   C¹³

4/4 | / / / / | / / / / | / / / / | / / / / |

G

| / / / / | / / / / |

Verse 1

G   C/G G
Is it a kind of dream,_____
Em   C   G
Floating out on the tide,_____
D   D/C   G   C
Following the river of death downstream?
       Am   D
Oh, is it a dream?

Verse 2

            G   C/G G
There's a fog along the hori - - zon,
   Em   C   G
A strange glow in the sky._____
      D   D/C   G   C
And nobody seems to know where you go.
           B
And what does it mean?
Edim⁷ Dsus⁴ D⁷   G
Oh,_____ is it a dream?

      Bm   C   D   D/F♯
Bright eyes,   burning like fire.
      Bm   C   Am
Bright eyes,   how can you close and fail?
B^7 Em   D/F♯   G
How can the light that burned so brightly
C   Am
Suddenly burn so pale?
D^7 G
Bright eyes.

ink

    G   Em   C
| (eyes.) / / / | / / / / / | / / / / / |

erse 3

G   C/G   G
Is it a kind of sha - - dow,
Em   C   G
Reaching into the night,____
D   D/C   G   C
Wandering over the hills unseen?
    Am   D
Or is it a dream?

erse 4

          G   C/G   G
There's a high wind in the trees,_____
    Em   C G
A cold sound in the air._____
    D   D/C   G   C
And nobody ever knows when you go.
               B
And where do you start,
$Edim^7$ $Dsus^4$ D^7 G
Oh,_____ into the dark?

Chorus 2

        Bm   C   D   D/F♯
Bright eyes,   burning like fire.
        Bm   C   Am
Bright eyes,   how can you close and fail?
B^7 Em   D/F♯   G
How can the light that burned so brightly
C   Am
Suddenly burn so pale?
D^7 G
Bright eyes.

Chorus 3

        Bm   C   D   D/F♯
Bright eyes,   burning like fire.
        Bm   C   Am
Bright eyes,   how can you close and fail?
B^7 Em   D/F♯   G
How can the light that burned so brightly
C   Am
Suddenly burn so pale?
D^7 G
Bright eyes.

Coda

        G
‖ (eyes.) / / / | / / / ‖

Cosmic Dancer

Words and Music by
MARC BOLAN

G   Em   F   C   Am   D7

♩ = 72

Verse 1

4/4 | G | Em
I was dancing when I was twelve,

| G | Em
I was dancing when I was twelve.

| F | C
I was dancing when I was aaah,

| F | C
I was dancing when I was aaah.

Verse 2

| G | Em
I danced myself right out the womb,

| G | Em
I danced myself right out the womb.

| F | C
Is it strange to dance so soon?

| F | C
I danced myself right out the womb.

Verse 3

| G | | Em |

I was dancing when I was eight,

| G | | Em |

I was dancing when I was eight.

| F | | C |

Is it strange to dance so late?

| F | | C |

Is it strange to dance so late?

| Am | | D⁷ |

Oh,___ oh, oh, oh.

Verse 4

| G | | Em |

I danced myself into the tomb,

| G | | Em |

I danced myself into the tomb.

| F | | C |

Is it strange to dance so soon?

| F | | C |

I danced myself into the tomb.

Verse 5

| G | | Em |

Is it wrong to understand

| G | | Em |

The fear that dwells inside a man?___

| F | | C |

What's it like to be a loon?

| F | | C |

I liken it to a balloon.

| Am | | D⁷ |

Oh,___ oh, oh, oh.

Verse 6

| G | Em

I danced myself out of the womb,

| G | Em

I danced myself out of the womb.

| F | C

Is it strange to dance so soon?

| F | C

I danced myself into the tomb.

And then again once more:

Verse 7

| G | Em

I danced myself out of the womb,

| G | Em

I danced myself out of the womb.

| F | C

Is it strange to dance so soon?

| F | C

I danced myself out of the womb.

| Am | D⁷

Oh,___ oh, oh, oh.

Coda

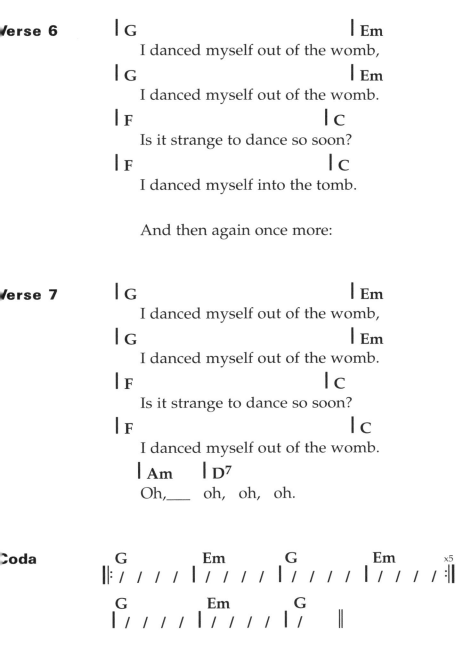

Cat's In The Cradle

Words and Music by
HARRY CHAPIN AND SANDY CHAPIN

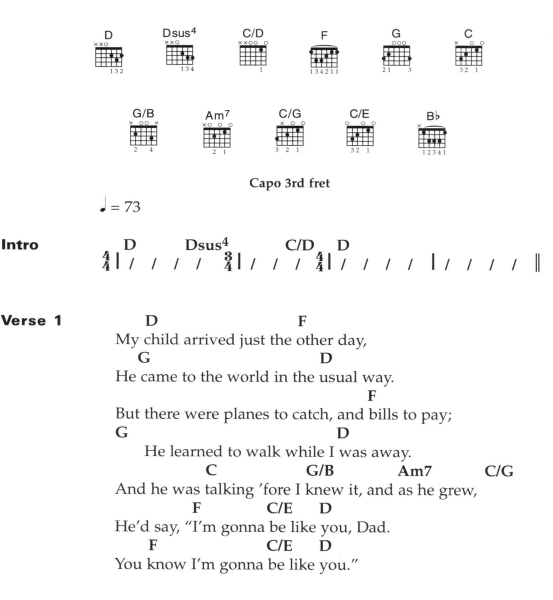

Capo 3rd fret

♩ = 73

Intro

| D | | | | Dsus⁴ | | | C/D | D | | | | | | | | |

Verse 1

     D   F
My child arrived just the other day,
   G   D
He came to the world in the usual way.
                F
But there were planes to catch, and bills to pay;
G   D
   He learned to walk while I was away.
      C   G/B   Am7   C/G
And he was talking 'fore I knew it, and as he grew,
     F   C/E   D
He'd say, "I'm gonna be like you, Dad.
    F   C/E   D
You know I'm gonna be like you."

         D   **C**
And the cat's in the cradle and the silver spoon,
F   **G**
Little boy blue and the man in the moon.
 D   **C**
"When you coming home, Dad?" "I don't know when,
    F   **C/E**   **D**
But we'll get together then.___
     F   **C/E**   **D**
You know we'll have a good time then."

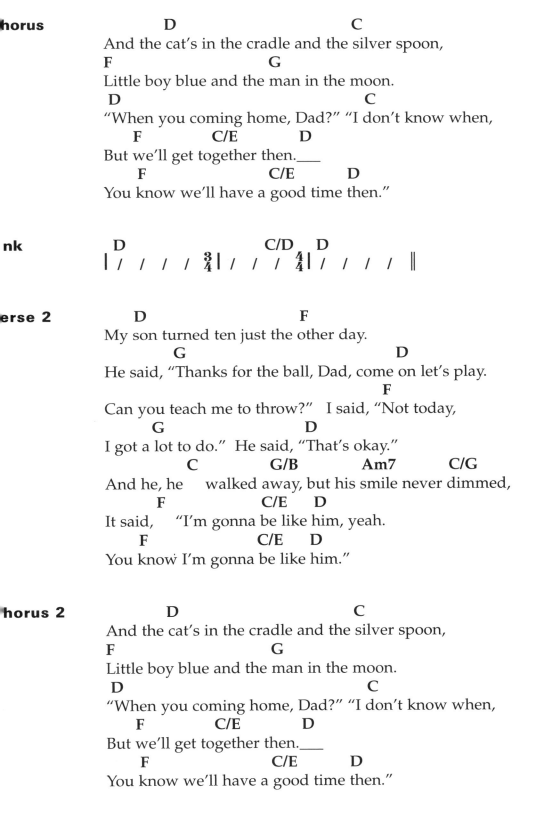

     D   **F**
My son turned ten just the other day.
       G   **D**
He said, "Thanks for the ball, Dad, come on let's play.
                          F
Can you teach me to throw?" I said, "Not today,
     G   **D**
I got a lot to do." He said, "That's okay."
       C   **G/B**   **Am7**   **C/G**
And he, he   walked away, but his smile never dimmed,
     F   **C/E**   **D**
It said,   "I'm gonna be like him, yeah.
    F   **C/E**   **D**
You know I'm gonna be like him."

        D   **C**
And the cat's in the cradle and the silver spoon,
F   **G**
Little boy blue and the man in the moon.
 D   **C**
"When you coming home, Dad?" "I don't know when,
    F   **C/E**   **D**
But we'll get together then.___
     F   **C/E**   **D**
You know we'll have a good time then."

Link

D   C/D   D

| / / / / / $\frac{3}{4}$ | / / / / $\frac{4}{4}$ | / / / / ‖

Verse 3

               D   F
Well, he came from college just the other day,
    G   D
So much like a man I just had to say
                                            F
"Son, I'm proud of you. Can you sit for a while?"
     G   D
He shook his head, and he said with a smile,
                  C   G/B   Am7   C/G
"What I'd really like, Dad, is to borrow the car keys.
F   C/E   D
    See you later. Can I have them please?"

Chorus 3

             D   C
And the cat's in the cradle and the silver spoon,
F   G
Little boy blue and the man in the moon.
  D   C
"When you coming home, son?" "I don't know when,
    F   C/E   D
But we'll get together then.___
      F   C/E   D
You know we'll have a good time then."

Link

B♭   C Am⁷ D   B♭   C Am⁷

| / / / / | / / / / | / / / / |

D

| / / / / | / / / / ‖

Verse 4

D   F

I've long since retired, my son's moved away.

G   D

I called him up just the other day.

                                      F

I said, "I'd like to see you if you don't mind."

                    G   D

He said, "I'd love to, Dad, if I could find the time.

                      C   G/B   Am7   C/G

You see, my new job's a hassle, and the kids have the flu,

               F   C/E   D

But it's sure nice talking to you, Dad.

               F   C/E   D

It's been sure nice talking to you."

Verse 5

                      C   G/B   Am7   C/G

And as I hung up the phone, it occurred to me,

             F   C/E   D

He'd grown up just like me.

             F   C/E   D

My boy was just like me.

Chorus 4

                  D   C

And the cat's in the cradle and the silver spoon,

F   G

Little boy blue and the man in the moon.

D   C

"When you coming home, son?" "I don't know when,

              F   C/E   D

But we'll get together then.___

             F   C/E   D

You know we'll have a good time then."

(freely, slower)

Coda

D   Dsus^4 D   C/D D

| / / / / / | / / / ‖

Chestnut Mare

Words and Music by
ROGER McGUINN AND JACQUES LEVY

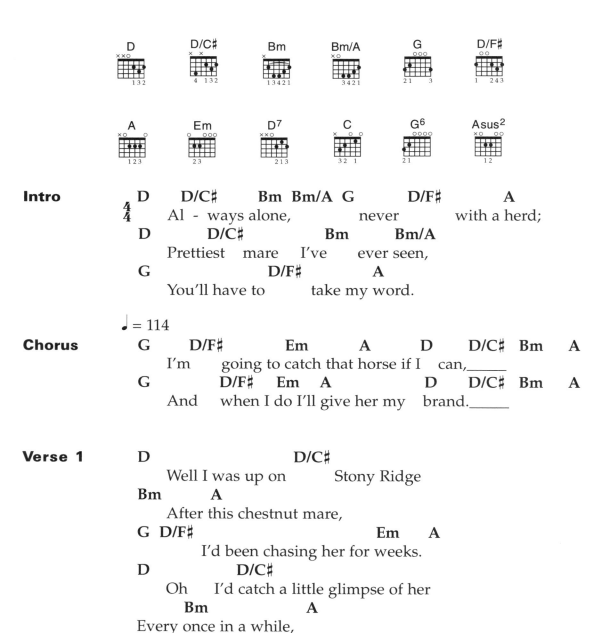

Intro

D   D/C♯   Bm Bm/A G   D/F♯   A
4/4   Al - ways alone,   never   with a herd;
D   D/C♯   Bm   Bm/A
Prettiest mare   I've   ever seen,
G   D/F♯   A
You'll have to   take my word.

♩ = 114

Chorus

G   D/F♯   Em   A   D   D/C♯ Bm   A
I'm   going to catch that horse if I   can,_____
G   D/F♯ Em A   D   D/C♯ Bm   A
And   when I do I'll give her my   brand._____

Verse 1

D   D/C♯
Well I was up on   Stony Ridge
Bm   A
After this chestnut mare,
G D/F♯   Em   A
I'd been chasing her for weeks.
D   D/C♯
Oh   I'd catch a little glimpse of her
Bm   A
Every once in a while,
G   D/F♯   A
Taking her meal or bathing,   fine lady.

          D D/C♯   Bm   A
This one day I happened to be real close to her
                        G   D/F♯
And I saw her standing over there,
Em   A   D   D/C♯
So I snuck up on her nice and easy,
Bm   A   G D/F♯   Em   A
Got my rope out   and I flung it in the air!

Chorus 2   G   D/F♯   Em   A   D   D/C♯ Bm   A
I'm   going to catch that horse if I   can,_____
              G   D/F♯ Em A   D   D/C♯ Bm   A
And   when I do I'll give her my   brand._____
              G   D/F♯   Em
And we'll be friends for life,
              G   D/F♯   Em
She'll be just like a wife.
              G   D/F♯   Em   A   D   D/C♯ Bm A
I'm   going to   catch that horse if I   can._____

Verse 2   D   D/C♯   Bm
Well I got her,   and I'm pulling on her,
                      A   G   D/F♯   Em A
And she's pulling back like this mule going up a ladder.
D   D/C♯   Bm   A
And I take a choice, and I jump right up on her.
G   D/F♯   Em
Damned if I don't land right on top of her!
A   D   D/C♯   Bm   A
And she takes off,   running up onto the ridge,
               G   ·   D/F♯   A
Higher than I've ever been before.

```
                              D        D/C♯
She's running along just      fine,
Bm              A
    Till she stops,          something spooked her,
G                D/F♯                         Em              A
    It's a sidewinder, all coiled  and   ready to strike.
D  D/C♯  Bm                                      A
               She doesn't know what to do for a second
           G                 D/F♯           Em                A
But then        she jumps off the edge…        me holding on!
```

Bridge

```
D⁷                             C          Bm              Em
    Above the hills        higher than eagles were gliding
    G⁶            D
Suspended in the sky,
D⁷                             C              Bm              Em
Over the moon,         straight for the sun we were riding;
    G⁶          D/F♯         Asus²
My eyes were filled with light.
    D⁷                          C         Bm              Em
Behind us black walls, below us a bottomless canyon
G⁶                     D
Floating with no sound.
D⁷                  C              Bm          Em
Gulls far below, seemed to be suddenly rising
G⁶          D/F♯  Asus²
Exploding all   around.
```

Chorus 3

```
G     D/F♯         Em        A        D      D/C♯  Bm    A
  I'm    going to catch that horse if I    can,_____
G           D/F♯   Em    A            D          D/C♯  Bm    A
  And    when I do I'll give her my      brand._____
G         D/F♯     Em
  And we'll be friends for life,
G           D/F♯   Em
  She'll be just like a wife.
G         D/F♯         Em              A        D      D/C♯  Bm   A
  I'm     going to    catch that horse if I   can._____
```

40

Verse 3
```
         D                   D/C♯      Bm                        A
         And we were falling          down this crevice,
         G                           D/F♯   Em    A
         About a mile down, I'd say,
                             D                D/C♯
         I look down and I see this red thing below us
         Bm                    A
         Coming up real fast
                         G            D/F♯                    Em
         And it's our reflection in this          little pool of water
                         A        D           D/C♯
         About six  feet wide and one foot deep.
         Bm                        A        G         D/F♯
         And we're falling down right through it,
                 Em                        A
         And we hit and we splashed it dry.
         D                   D/C♯         Bm                   A
         That's when I lost my hold          and she got away.
         G                             D/F♯   Em          A
         But I'm gonna try to get her again some day.
```

Chorus 4
```
         G    D/F♯       Em       A      D     D/C♯ Bm    A
         I'm     going to catch that horse if I    can,_____
         G         D/F♯   Em   A        D          D/C♯ Bm    A
         And    when I do I'll give her my     brand._____
         G      D/F♯    Em
         And we'll be friends for life,
         G        D/F♯    Em
         She'll be just like a wife.
         G      D/F♯     Em        A
         I'm going to catch that horse,
         G      D/F♯         Em         A
         I'm      going to catch that horse,
         G      D/F♯    Em       A      D        D/C♯  Bm     A
         I'm going to catch that horse if I    can._____
         G  D/F♯       Em       A      G     D/F♯   Em   A    D
         I'm going to catch that horse if I can._____    ‖
```

Crazy Little Thing Called Love

Words and Music by
FREDDIE MERCURY

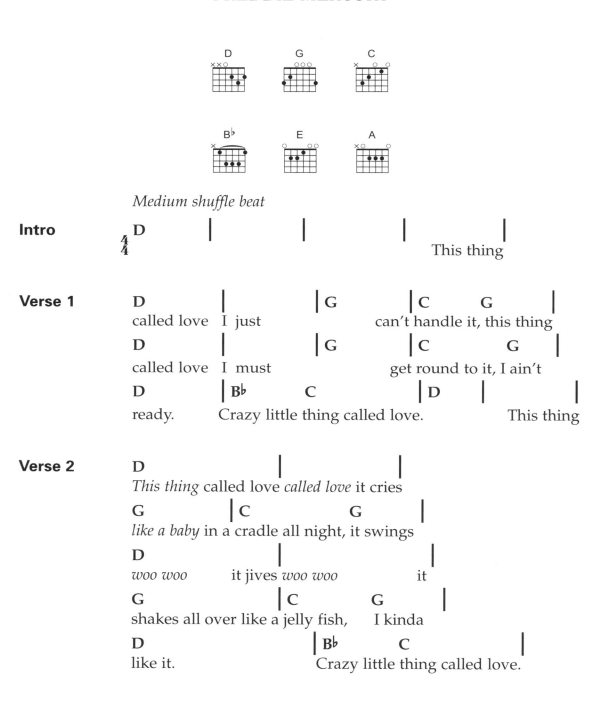

Medium shuffle beat

Intro $\frac{4}{4}$ D | | | |

This thing

Verse 1 D | |G |C   G |

called love   I just   can't handle it, this thing

D | |G |C   G |

called love   I must   get round to it, I ain't

D |B♭   C |D | |

ready.   Crazy little thing called love.   This thing

Verse 2 D | |

This thing called love *called love* it cries

G |C   G |

like a baby in a cradle all night, it swings

D | |

woo woo   it jives *woo woo*   it

G |C   G |

shakes all over like a jelly fish,   I kinda

D |B♭   C |

like it.   Crazy little thing called love.

```
         D                    |                        |
                                              There goes my

Chorus 1   |G          |       |C                |G              |
           baby,              she knows how to rock 'n' roll. She drives me
           Bb         |              |
           crazy            she gives me
           E          A         |F               |
           hot and cold fever, then she leaves me in a cool, cool sweat.
           N.C.            |              |E        |A          |
                                                I gotta be cool
```

```
Verse 3    D        |        |G         |C        G      |
                relax,    get hip,        get on my tracks, take a
           D               |         |
           backseat, hitch-hike,          and
           G                    |C       G      |
           take a long ride on my motorbike until I'm
           D         |Bb       C         |D      |           |
           ready.       Crazy little thing called love.    There goes my
```

Chorus 1   (as Chorus 1)

```
Verse 4    D          |         |G         |C        G      |
                relax,    get hip,        get on my tracks, take a
           D               |         |
           backseat, hitch-hike,          and
           G                    |C       G      |
           take a long ride on my motorbike until I'm
           D              |Bb       C            |
           ready. Ready Freddie. Crazy little thing called love.
           D            |              |
                                This thing
```

43

Verse 5

D | |G |C   G |
called love I just   can't handle it,   this thing

D | |G |C   G |
called love I must   get round to it, I ain't

D | Bb   C |D |
ready.   Crazy little thing called love.

Bb   C |D |
Crazy little thing called love,
(Repeat last two bars till fade)

Dancing In The Moonlight

Words and Music by
SHERMAN KELLY

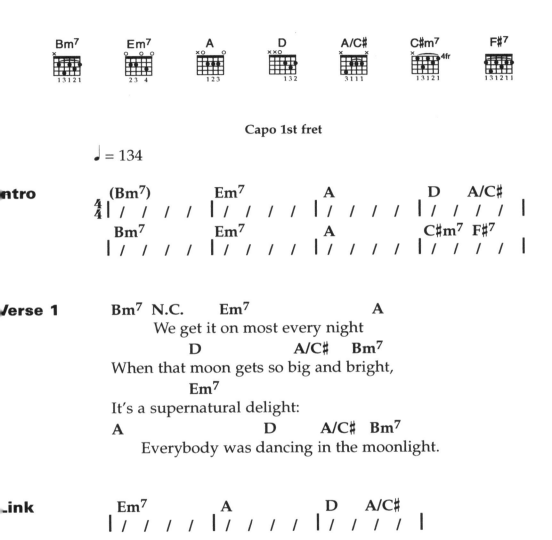

Bm7 Em7 A D A/C# C#m7 F#7

Capo 1st fret

♩ = 134

Intro

$\frac{4}{4}$

(Bm7)　　Em7　　　　A　　　　D　A/C#

Bm7　　Em7　　　　A　　　　C#m7 F#7

Verse 1

Bm7 N.C.　Em7　　　　　　A
　　We get it on most every night
　　　　D　　　　A/C#　Bm7
When that moon gets so big and bright,
　　　Em7
It's a supernatural delight:
A　　　　　　D　　A/C#　Bm7
　　Everybody was dancing in the moonlight.

Link

Em7　　　A　　　D　A/C#

Verse 2

Bm⁷ N.C.   Em⁷   A
     Everybody here is out of sight –
            D   A/C♯   Bm⁷
They don't bark and they don't bite;
                Em⁷
They keep things loose, they keep things light.
A   D   A/C♯ Bm⁷
     Everybody was dancing in the moonlight.

Chorus

Em⁷
Dancing in the moonlight,
A   D   A/C♯   Bm⁷
     Everybody's feeling warm and right.
       Em⁷
It's such a fine and natural sight:
A   D   A/C♯ Bm⁷
     Everybody's dancing in the moonlight.

Verse 3

          Em⁷   A
We like our fun and we never fight,
         D   A/C♯ Bm⁷
You can't dance and stay uptight.
       Em⁷
It's a supernatural delight:
A   D   A/C♯ Bm⁷
     Everybody was dancing in the moonlight.

Chorus 2

Em⁷
Dancing in the moonlight,
A   D   A/C♯   Bm⁷
     Everybody's feeling warm and right.
       Em⁷
It's such a fine and natural sight:
A   D   A/C♯ Bm⁷
     Everybody's dancing in the moonlight.

Guitar solo

Em⁷   A   D   A/C♯

| / / / / / | / / / / | / / / / |

Bm⁷   Em⁷   A   D   A/C♯

| / / / / / | / / / / | / / / / | / / / / |

Verse 4

Bm⁷ N.C.   Em⁷
     Everybody here is out of sight –

A   D   A/C♯   Bm⁷
   They don't bark and they don't bite;

            Em⁷
They keep things loose, they keep things light.

A   D   A/C♯   Bm⁷
   Everybody was dancing in the moonlight.

Chorus 3

Em⁷
Dancing in the moonlight,

A   D   A/C♯   Bm⁷
   Everybody's feeling warm and right.

      Em⁷
It's such a fine and natural sight:

A   D   A/C♯   Bm⁷
   Everybody's dancing in the moonlight.

Chorus 4

    Em⁷
‖: Dancing in the moonlight,

A   D   A/C♯   Bm⁷
   Everybody's feeling warm and right.

      Em⁷
It's such a fine and natural sight:

A   D   A/C♯   Bm⁷
   Everybody's dancing in the moonlight.   :‖ *repeat to fade*

47

Five Years

Words and Music by
DAVID BOWIE

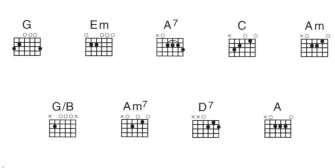

♩. = 48

Intro   **12/8** | *(drums fade in)*

Verse 1

| G

   Pushing through the market square,

| Em

   So many mothers sighing,

| A⁷

   News had just come over,

   | C

We had five years left to cry in.

| G

   News guy wept and told us,

| Em

Earth was really dying,

| A⁷

   Cried so much his face was wet,

   | C

Then I knew he was not lying.

Prechorus

|G

I heard telephones, opera house, favourite melodies.

   |Em

I saw boys, toys, electric irons and T.Vs.

  |A⁷

My brain hurt like a warehouse, it had no room to spare,

    |C

I had to cram so many things to store everything in there,

Bridge

          |Am

And all the fat-skinny people,

C |Am

And all the tall-short people,

C   G/B Am⁷|G

And all the no - bo - dy   people,

C |D⁷

And all the somebody people.

           |Am   C

I never thought I'd need so many people.

Verse 3

|G

A girl my age went off her head,

|Em

Hit some tiny children.

|A⁷

If the black hadn't-a pulled her off

|C

I think she would have killed them.

49

| G

A soldier with a broken arm

| Em

Fixed his stare to the wheels of a Cadillac;

| A⁷

A cop knelt and kissed the feet of a priest,

| C

And a queer threw up at the sight of that.

Verse 4 | G

I think I saw you in an ice cream parlour,

| Em

Drinking milk shakes cold and long,

| A

Smiling and waving and looking so fine.

| C

Don't think you knew you were in this song.

Prechorus 2 | G

And it was cold and it rained so I felt like an actor,

| Em

And I thought of Ma and I wanted to get back there –

| A

Your face, your race, the way that you talk;

| C

I kiss you, you're beautiful, I want you to walk.

Chorus

‖: **G**
We've got five years, stuck on my eyes.

| **Em**
Five years, what a surprise!

| **A**
We've got five years, my brain hurts a lot.

| **C**   :‖ x4
Five years, that's all we've got.

Coda 1

| **G**
Five years,

| **Em**
Five years,

| **A**
Five years,

| **C**
Five years!

Coda 2   **G**   *(drums to fade)*

| / / / / | / /   ‖

Fire And Rain

Words and Music by
JAMES TAYLOR

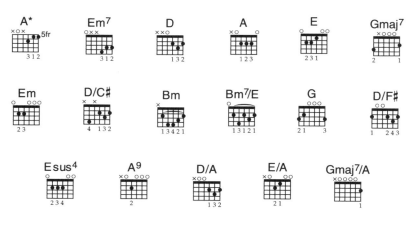

Capo 3rd fret

♩ = 74

Intro

$\frac{4}{4}$ | A* Em⁷ / / / / | D A / / / / | / / / / | E Gmaj⁷ / / / / ‖

Verse 1

A   Em   D   A
   Just yesterday morning they let me know you were gone___
       E   Gmaj⁷
Suzanne, the plans they made put an end to you.
A   Em   D   A
   I walked out this morning and I wrote down this song,___
      E   Gmaj⁷
I just can't remember who to send it to.

D D/C♯   Bm   Bm^7/E A
I've seen fire and I've seen rain,
       D   D/C♯   Bm   Bm^7/E   A
I've seen   sunny days that I thought would never end;___
       D   D/C♯   Bm   Bm^7/E   A
I've seen lonely times when I could not find a friend,
     G   D/F♯   Esus^4 Em   A^9
But I always thought that I'd see you   again.

         A   Em
Won't you look down upon me, Jesus,
       D   A
You gotta help me make a stand,
          E   Gmaj^7
You just got to see me through another day.
A   Em   D   A
  My body's aching and my time is at hand,
       E   Gmaj^7
And I won't make it any other way.

D D/C♯   Bm   Bm^7/E A
I've seen fire and I've seen rain,
       D   D/C♯   Bm   Bm^7/E   A
I've seen   sunny days that I thought would never end;___
       D   D/C♯   Bm   Bm^7/E   A
I've seen lonely times when I could not find a friend,
     G   D/F♯   Esus^4 Em   A^9
But I always thought that I'd see you   again.

        A   A^9
Been walking my mind to an easy time,
    D/A   A
My back turned towards the sun,
               E/A
Lord knows, when the cold wind blows
    Gmaj^7/A
It'll turn your head around.

                              A   A⁹
              Well there's hours of time on the telephone line
                 D/A   A
              To talk about things to come,____
                                   E/A   Gmaj⁷/A
              Sweet dreams and flying machines in pieces on the ground.

Chorus 3   D   D/C♯   Bm   Bm⁷/E   A
                    I've seen fire and I've seen rain,
                        D   D/C♯   Bm   Bm⁷/E   A
              I've seen   sunny days that I thought would never end;____
                        D   D/C♯   Bm   Bm⁷/E   A
              I've seen lonely times when I could not find a friend,
                    G   D/F♯   Esus⁴   Em
              But I always thought that I'd see you, baby,
              A⁹
                    One more time again, now.

Coda

                 Thought I'd see you one more time again

                 There's just a few things coming my way

                 This time around, now

                 Thought I'd see you, thought I'd see you,

                 Fire and rain, now.   ‖

Gallows Pole

Words and Music by
JIMMY PAGE AND ROBERT PLANT

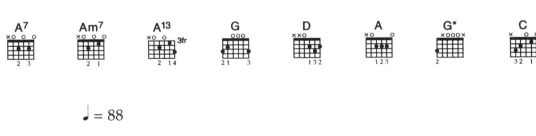

A7   Am7   A13   G   D   A   G*   C

♩ = 88

Intro

4/4 ‖: A7   Am7 A13 A7   Am7 A13 x4 :‖

Verse 1

A7   Am7   A13 A7   Am7   A13
Hangman,   hangman,   hold it a little while,
A7   Am7   A13
   I think I see my friends coming,
G   D   A7   Am7   A13
   Riding many a mile.

Link

| A7   Am7 A13 |
‖ / / / / |

Verse 2

A7   Am7   A13
   Friends, did you get some silver?
A7   Am7   A13
   Did you get a little gold?
A7   Am7   A13
   What did you bring me, my dear friends,
G   D   A7   Am7 A13 A7 Am7
Keep me from the gallows   pole?
        A13   A7
What did you bring me
        G   D   A7   Am7 A13
To keep me from the gallows   pole?

Link 2
```
    A⁷      Am⁷  A¹³
| /   /   /   /   |
```

Verse 3
```
    A⁷                    Am⁷  A¹³  A⁷                   Am⁷   A¹³
   I couldn't get no silver,      I couldn't get no gold,
    A⁷                      Am⁷            A¹³
   You know that we're too damn poor
         G                 D        A⁷      Am⁷  A¹³
   To    keep you from the gallows      pole.
```

Link 3
```
    A⁷      Am⁷   A¹³
| /   /   /   /   |
```

Verse 4
```
    A        G      D      G A            D    G
   Hangman,      hangman,      hold it a little while,
    A        G      D         G
     I think I see my    brother coming,
            D        G      A  G   A
   Riding many  a   mile.
```

Link 4
```
    G* A  G* A
| /     /     /  /  |
```

Verse 5
```
    G*    A          G*  A
   Brother, did you get me some silver?
    G*            A    G* A
      Did you get a lit - tle gold?
    G*    A  G*  A
      What did you bring me, my brother,
         G                  D       G* A   G*  A
   To keep me from the gallows      pole?
```

Link 5
```
    G* A  G* A
| /     /     /  /  |
```

56

Verse 6

G*   A   G*   A
Brother, I brought you some silver, yeah,
G*   A   G*   A
   I brought a little gold,
G*   A   G*   A
   I brought a lit - tle of everything
   G   D   G* A   G* A
To keep you from the gallows   pole.
  G* A   G* A
| /   /   /   / |
           C   D   G*   A   G*   A
Yes,   I brought you to keep you from the gallows pole.

Link 6

   G* A   G* A
| /   /   /   / |

Verse 7

A   G   D   G A   G   D
Hangman,   hangman,   turn your head awhile,
A   G   D   G   D   G*   A G* A
   I think I see my sister coming, riding many a mile,___
          G*   A G* A
Mile, mile, mile.

Link 7

   G* A
| /   /   /   / |

Verse 8

G* A   G*   A
Sister, I implore you, take him by the hand,
G*   A
Take him to some shady bower,
G   D   G*   A
Save me from the wrath of this man.
G* A   G*   A G   D   G* A
   Please take him, save me from the wrath of this man, man.

Link 8

G* A G* A
| /   /   / / |

Verse 9

A   G   D   G   A   D   G
Hangman,   hangman,   upon your face a smile,
A   G   D   G
Tell me that I'm free to ride,
              D   G* A   G* A G* A
Ride for many mile, mile, mile.

Link 9

G* A G* A
| /   /   / / |

Verse 10

  G* A G* A   G*   A G*   A
Oh yes, you got a fine sister, she warmed my blood from cold,
    G*   A G*   A
She warmed my blood to boiling hot
   G   D   G* A   G* A
To keep you from the gallows   pole,   pole,
    G* A   G* A
Pole, pole,   yeah, yeah.

Verse 9

    G* A G*   A   G* A G*   A
Your brother brought me silver, and your sis-ter warmed my soul
    G* A G*   A
But now I laugh   and pull so hard
        G   D   G*   A
See you swinging on the gallows   pole, yeah.
  G* A G* A
| /   /   / / |

    G* A G*   A
But now I laugh   and pull so hard
            G   D   G*   A G* A
And see you swinging on the gallows   pole, pole, pole.
  G D G* A G* A
| / / /   / |

```
         G              D        G*     A  G* A  x3
||: Swinging on the gallows pole!                    :||
   G              D         G*  A  G*  A
   Swinging on the gallows     pole,    pole,
   G        D       G*      A  G*  A
      Pole,    pole, pole,
   G        D       G*     A  G* A   G   D
      Pole,    pole, yeah!
```

Coda
```
              G* A  G* A  G   D
     ||:/       /       /    /   :||  repeat vocal ad lib. to fade
```

Get It On

Words and Music by
MARC BOLAN

E   A   G   Am

♩ = 120

Intro

E
4/4 / / / / | / / / / | / / / /   / / / /

Verse 1

| | E | A
Well you're dirty and sweet, clad in black,
                        | E
Don't look back and I love you,
            | A | E
You're dirty and sweet, oh yeah.
| |
Well you're slim and you're weak,
                    | A | E
You've got the teeth of the Hydra upon you,
            | A | E
You're dirty sweet and you're my girl.

Chorus

| | G | Am | E
Get it on, bang a gong, get it on.
| | G | Am | E | |
Get it on, bang a gong, get it on.   / / / / / / / / / / / /

Verse 2

| | E
Well you're built like a car –
   | A | E
You got a hubcap diamond star halo,
  | A | E
You're built like a car, oh yeah.
| | | A
Well you're an untamed youth, that's the truth,
    | E
With your cloak full of eagles,
  | A | E
You're dirty sweet and you're my girl.

Chorus 2

| | G | Am | E
Get it on, bang a gong, get it on.
| | G | Am | E | |
Get it on, bang a gong, get it on.   / / / / / / / / / / / /

Verse 3

| | E
Well you're windy and wild –
  | A | E
You got the blues in your shoes and your stockings,
 | A | E
You're windy and wild, oh yeah.
| | E
Well you're built like a car –
  | A | E
You got a hubcap diamond star halo,
 | A | E
You're dirty sweet and you're my girl.

Chorus 3 | | G | Am | E

Get it on, bang a gong, get it on.

| | G | Am | E |

Get it on, bang a gong, get it on.   / / / / / / / /

Link   E

‖: / / / / | / / / / | / / / / :‖ / / / /

Verse 4 | | E | A

Well you're dirty and sweet, clad in black,

| E

Don't look back and I love you,

| A | E

You're dirty and sweet, oh yeah.

| |

Well, you dance when you walk

| A | E

So let's dance, take a chance, understand me,

| A | E

You're dirty sweet and you're my girl.

Chorus 4 | | G | Am | E

Get it on, bang a gong, get it on.

| | G | Am | E

Get it on, bang a gong, get it on.

| | G | Am | E |

Get it on, bang a gong, get it on.   / / / / / / / /

Link 2   E

‖: / / / / | / / / / | / / / / :‖ / / / /

Chorus 5   ‖: |G |Am |E   x3 :‖

Get it on, bang a gong, get it on.   / / / /

| |G |Am |E

Get it on, bang a gong, right on!

|

Take me!

Guitar solo |G |Am |E | |

/ / / /   / / / /   / / / /   / / / /   / / / /

Coda | | | |E | *(fade)*

Well,   meanwhile I'm still thinking…   / / / /

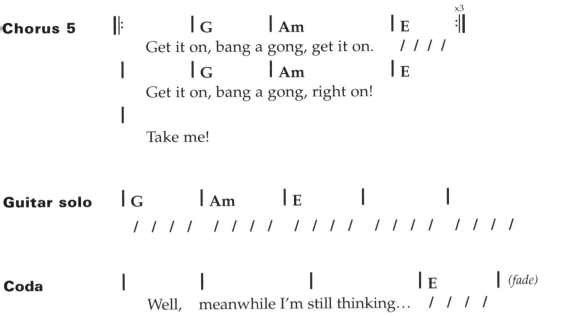

The Guitar Man

Words and Music by
DAVID GATES

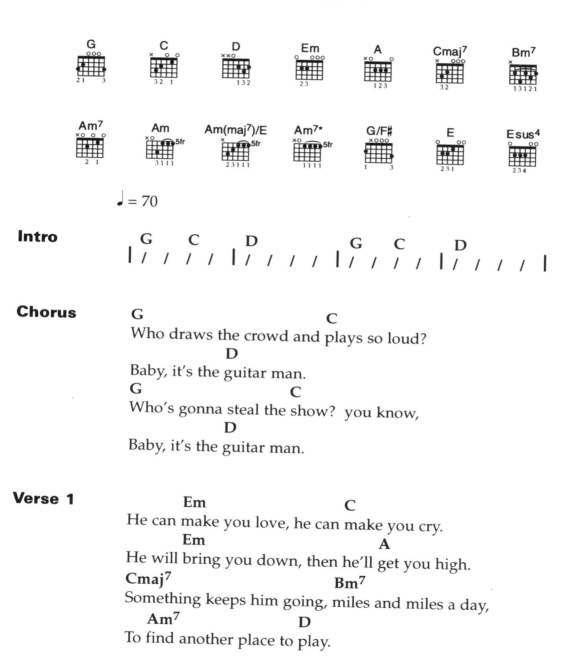

♩ = 70

Intro

G C D | G C D

| / / / / | / / / / | / / / / | / / / / |

Chorus

G   C
Who draws the crowd and plays so loud?
          D
Baby, it's the guitar man.
G   C
Who's gonna steal the show? you know,
          D
Baby, it's the guitar man.

Verse 1

       Em   C
He can make you love, he can make you cry.
       Em   A
He will bring you down, then he'll get you high.
Cmaj⁷   Bm⁷
Something keeps him going, miles and miles a day,
   Am⁷   D
To find another place to play.

Chorus 2

G   C
Night after night who treats you right?
        D
Baby, it's the guitar man.
G   C
Who's on the radio? You go to listen
      D
To the guitar man.

Verse 2

      Em   C
Then he comes to town, and you see his face,
      Em   A
And you think you might like to take his place.
Cmaj^7 Bm^7
Something keeps him drifting miles and miles away,
Am^7 D
Searching for the songs to play.

Bridge

N.C. Am   Am(maj^7)/E Am^{7*} D
Then you listen to the music and you like to sing along,
G   G/F♯   Em   E
You want to get the meaning out of each and every song.
      Am   Am(maj^7)/E
Then you find yourself a message
      Am^{7*} D
And some words to call your own___
        E   Esus^4 Cmaj^7
And take them home.

Guitar solo

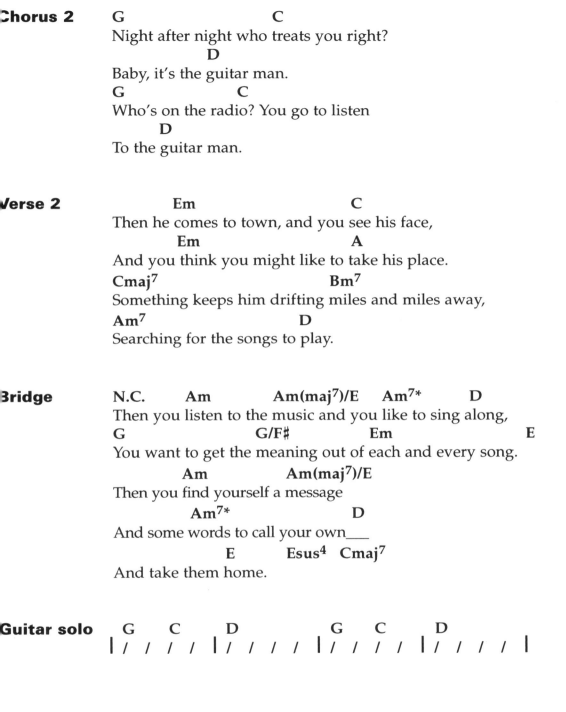

G C   D   G C   D
| / / / / | / / / / | / / / / | / / / / |

Verse 3

        Em   C
He can make you love, he can get you high.
        Em   A
He will bring you down, then he'll make you cry.
Cmaj^7 Bm^7
Something keeps him moving, but no-one seems to know
Am^7 D
What it is that makes him go.

Bridge 2

N.C.   Am   Am(maj^7)/E   Am^{7*} D
Then the lights begin to flicker and the sound is getting dim,
     G   G/F♯   Em   E
The voice begins to falter and the crowds are getting thin.
     Am   Am(maj^7)/E   Am^{7*}
But he never seems to notice – he's just got to find
   D   E   Esus^4 Cmaj^7
Another place to play,

Coda

     E   Cmaj^7 E   Cmaj^7
Fade away   got to play,
     E   Cmaj^7 E   Cmaj^7
Fade away   got to play.
E | Cmaj^7 ‖ *fade*

Happy

Words and Music by
MICK JAGGER AND KEITH RICHARDS

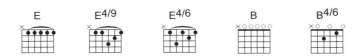

E-based chords are at the 5th fret from capo, actual 9th fret. Chords given are at actual pitch.
Open G tuning D G D G B D, capo IV.

♩ = 130

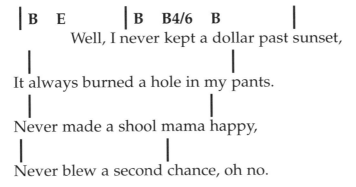

Verse 1

| B E | B B4/6 B | |

Well, I never kept a dollar past sunset,

It always burned a hole in my pants.

Never made a shool mama happy,

Never blew a second chance, oh no.

Chorus 1

| E   E4/9 | E4/6   E |

I need a love to keep me happy,

| E4/9 | E4/6   E |

I need a love to keep me happy.

| B   E | B   E |

Baby,   baby keep me happy.

| B   E | B   E |

Baby,   baby keep me happy.

Verse 2

| B   B4/6 B |

Always took candy from strangers,

Didn't wanna get me no trade.

Never want to be like papa,

Working for the boss every night and day.

Chorus 2

| E   E4/9 | E4/6   E

I need a love to keep me happy,

| E4/9 | E4/6   E | B   E

I need a love, baby won't you keep me happy.

| B   E | B   E

Baby,   baby keep me happy.

| B   E

Baby, please keep me.

Link solo

B   E   B   E   B   E

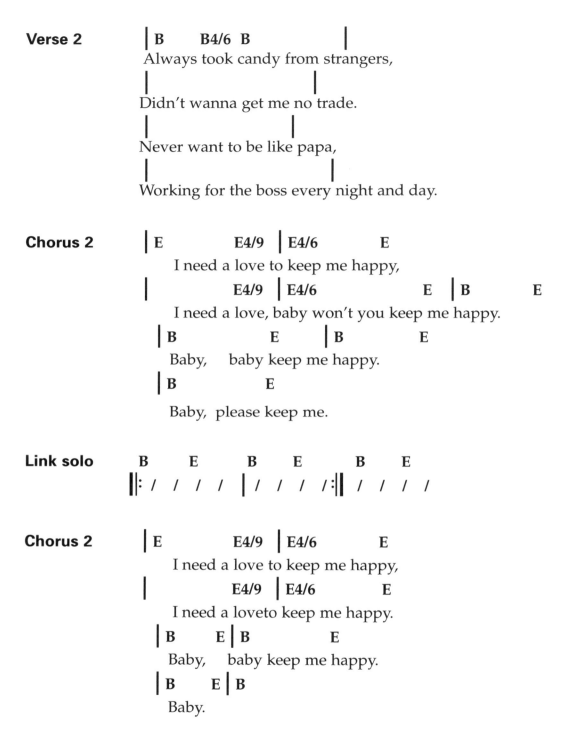

Chorus 2

| E   E4/9 | E4/6   E

I need a love to keep me happy,

| E4/9 | E4/6   E

I need a loveto keep me happy.

| B   E | B   E

Baby,   baby keep me happy.

| B   E | B

Baby.

Verse 3

|B   B4/6 B |
Never got a flash out of cocktails

| |
When I got some flesh off the bone.

| |
Never got a lift out of Lear jets,

| |
When I can fly way back home.

Chorus 2

|E   E4/9 |E4/6   E
I need a love to keep me happy,

| E4/9 |E4/6   E
I need a love to keep me happy.

|B   E|B   E
Baby,   baby keep me happy.

|B   E|B   E
Baby,   baby keep me happy.

|B
Baby!

Coda solo

E   E4/9 |E4/6   E | E   E4/9 |E4/6   E
/ / / / / / / / / / / / / / / /

‖: B   E |B   E   :‖ *repeat ad lib to fade*
Happy,   Baby, won't you keep me

Harvest For The World

Words and Music by
O'KELLY ISLEY, MARVIN ISLEY, RONALD ISLEY,
RUDOLPH ISLEY, ERNIE ISLEY AND **CHRIS JASPER**

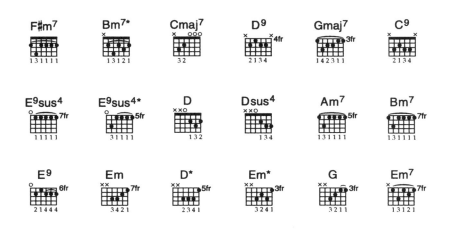

$\quad$ = 124

Intro

$\dfrac{4}{4}$ | F#m⁷ / / / / | Bm⁷* / / / / | Cmaj⁷ / / / / | / / / / |

||: D⁹ Gmaj⁷ / / / | C⁹ / / / / :|| D⁹ Gmaj⁷ / / / |

| E⁹sus⁴ E⁹sus⁴* / / | Cmaj⁷ / / / / | D Dsus⁴ D / / / ||

Verse 1

Am⁷   Bm⁷   E⁹sus⁴   E⁹
All babies together,   everyone a seed.
Am⁷   Bm⁷   E⁹sus⁴   E⁹   D* Em* G
Half of us are satisfied,   half of us in need.
Am⁷   Bm⁷   E⁹sus⁴   E⁹
Love's bountiful in us,   tarnished by our greed.
    Am⁷   D⁹   Gmaj⁷   C⁹
Oh, when will there be a harvest for the world?
     D⁹   Gmaj⁷   C⁹
Yeah, yeah,   yeah, yeah.

Link

D^9 $Gmaj^7$
Yeah.____

E^9sus^4 E^9sus^{4*} $Cmaj^7$ D $Dsus^4$ D
| /   /   /   /   / | /   /   /   / | /   /   /   / ||

Verse 2

Am^7 Bm^7 E^9sus^4 E^9
   A nation planted,   so concerned with gain,
Am^7 Bm^7 E^9sus^4 Em $D*$ $Em*$ G
As the seasons come and go, greater grows the pain.
     Am^7 Bm^7 E^9sus^4 E^9
And far   too many   feeling the strain.
     Am^7 D^9 $Gmaj^7$ C^9
Oh, when will there be a harvest for the world?
     D^9 $Gmaj^7$ C^9
Yeah,   yeah.

Link 2

D^9 $Gmaj^7$
Yeah.____

E^9sus^4 E^9sus^{4*} $Cmaj^7$ D $Dsus^4$ D
| /   /   /   /   / | /   /   /   / | /   /   /   / ||

Bridge

Em^7 Bm^7 Em^7 Am^7
Gather every man,   gather every woman;
Em^7 Bm^7 Em^7 Am^7 Bm^7
Celebrate your lives,   give thanks for your children, oh!
Em^7 Bm^7 Em^7 Am^7
Gather everyone,   gather all together
Em^7 Bm^7
Overlooking none   (overlooking none),
Em^7 Am^7 D^9 $Gmaj^7$ C^9
Hoping life gets better for the world.
     D^9 $Gmaj^7$ C^9
Yeah,   yeah, yeah.

Link 3

D^9　　　　$Gmaj^7$
Yeah.____

E^9sus^4　E^9sus^{4*}　　$Cmaj^7$　　　　　　　D　　$Dsus^4$　D
| / 　/ 　/ 　/ 　/ 　| / 　/ 　/ 　/ 　/ 　| / 　/ 　　/ 　　/ 　‖

Verse 3

Am^7　　　　　　　Bm^7　　　　　　　E^9sus^4　　　E^9
Dress me up for battle　　　when all I want is peace.
Am^7　　　　　　　Bm^7
Those of us who pay the price
E^9sus^4　　　　　　　Em　　D*　Em*　G
Come home with the least.
　　　Am^7　　　　　　　Bm^7　E^9sus^4　　　E^9
And　　　nation after nation turning into beast.
　　　Am^7　　　　　　　D^9　　　　　　　　　　$Gmaj^7$　C^9
Oh,　when will there be a harvest for the world?
　　　D^9　　$Gmaj^7$　C^9
Yeah, yeah.
　　　　　　D^9　　$Gmaj^7$　C^9
When will there be?
　　　　　D^9　　　　$Gmaj^7$　C^9
I wanna know now, now.

Coda

　　　　　　　　　　D^9　　$Gmaj^7$　　　C^9
‖: When will there be　　　　　a　harvest? :‖ *repeat ad lib. to end*
　　　　　　　　(harvest for the world)

Hymn

Words and Music by
JOHN LEES

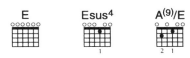

Open E tuning
(E B E G♯ B E)

$\quad \boldsymbol{\downarrow} = 67$

Intro

$\frac{4}{4}$ | E Esus⁴ E Esus⁴ / / / / | E Esus⁴ / / / / | E Esus⁴ / / / / | E Esus⁴ / / / / |

Chorus

   E   A⁽⁹⁾/E   E
  Valley's deep and the mountain's so high,
  A⁽⁹⁾/E
If you want to see God
              E Esus⁴
You've got to move on the other side.
E   A⁽⁹⁾/E   E
  You stand up there with your head in the clouds,
  A⁽⁹⁾/E   E
Don't try to fly, you know you might not come down.
  A⁽⁹⁾/E   E
Don't try to fly, dear God, you might not come down.
  E Esus⁴ E Esus⁴
| (down.) / / | / / / / |

Verse 1

```
E                              A⁽⁹⁾/E              E
     Jesus came down from Heaven to earth,
     A⁽⁹⁾/E                      E      Esus⁴
The people said it was a virgin birth.
E                              A⁽⁹⁾/E              E
     Jesus came down from Heaven to earth,
     A⁽⁹⁾/E                      E
The people said it was a virgin birth.
     A⁽⁹⁾/E                          E
The people said it was        a virgin birth.
   E      Esus⁴    E     Esus⁴
| (birth.)  /  /  |  /  /  /  /  |
```

Verse 2

```
E                              A⁽⁹⁾/E      E
     He told great stories of the Lord
     A⁽⁹⁾/E                      E      Esus⁴
And said he was the saviour of us all.
E                              A⁽⁹⁾/E      E
     He told great stories of the Lord
     A⁽⁹⁾/E                          E
And said he was the saviour of us all.
     A⁽⁹⁾/E                              E
And said he was the saviour        of us all.
   E    Esus⁴    E     Esus⁴
| (all.)  /  /  |  /  /  /  /  |
```

Verse 3

```
E                              A⁽⁹⁾/E              E
     For this we killed him, and nailed him up high.
     A⁽⁹⁾/E                      E      Esus⁴
He rose again as if to ask us why?
E                          A⁽⁹⁾/E      E
     Then he ascended into the sky
     A⁽⁹⁾/E                      E
As if to say in God alone you soar,
     A⁽⁹⁾/E                              E
As if to say in God        alone we fly.
   E    Esus⁴    E     Esus⁴
| (fly.)  /  /  |  /  /  /  /  |
```

Chorus 2

```
E                              A⁽⁹⁾/E                E
    Valley's deep and the mountain's so high,
        A⁽⁹⁾/E
    If you want to see God
                                        E   Esus⁴
    You've got to move on the other side.
E                                  A⁽⁹⁾/E              E
    You stand up there with your head in the clouds,
        A⁽⁹⁾/E                                E
    Don't try to fly, you know you might not come down.
        A⁽⁹⁾/E                                    E
    Don't try to fly, dear God,      you might not come down.
    E       Esus⁴    E    Esus⁴
  |(down.)  /   /  | /  /  /  /  |
```

Chorus 3

```
E                              A⁽⁹⁾/E                E
    Valley's deep and the mountain's so high,
        A⁽⁹⁾/E
    If you want to see God
                                        E   Esus⁴
    You've got to move on the other side.
E                                  A⁽⁹⁾/E              E
    You stand up there with your head in the clouds,
        A⁽⁹⁾/E                                E
    Don't try to fly, you know you might not come down.
        A⁽⁹⁾/E                                    E
    Don't try to fly, dear God,      you might not come down.
    E       Esus⁴    E    Esus⁴
  |(down.)  /   /  | /  /  /  /  |
```

Coda

```
    E    Esus⁴    E    Esus⁴ ×4 E    Esus⁴    E
  ||: /  /  /  /  | /  /  /  / :|| /  /  /  /  | /  ||
```

A Horse With No Name

Words and Music by
DEWEY BUNNELL

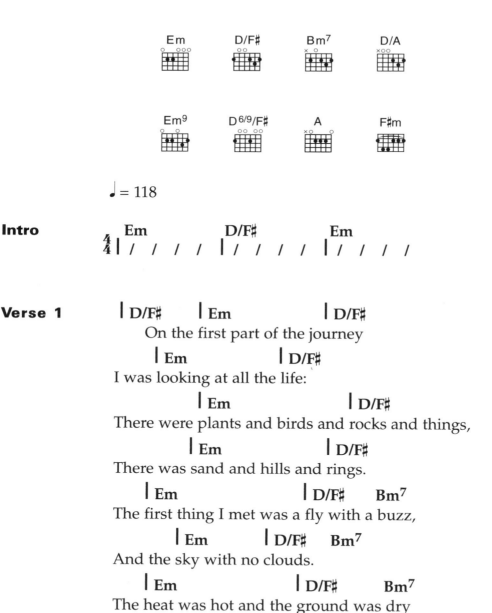

♩ = 118

Intro

$\frac{4}{4}$ | Em / / / / | D/F# / / / / | Em / / / /

Verse 1

| D/F# | Em | D/F#
On the first part of the journey
| Em | D/F#
I was looking at all the life:
| Em | D/F#
There were plants and birds and rocks and things,
| Em | D/F#
There was sand and hills and rings.
| Em | D/F#   Bm7
The first thing I met was a fly with a buzz,
| Em | D/F#   Bm7
And the sky with no clouds.
| Em | D/F#   Bm7
The heat was hot and the ground was dry
| Em | D/F#   D/A
But the air was full of sound.

Chorus

| Em^9 | D$^{6/9}$/F$\sharp$

I've been through the desert on a horse with no name,

| Em^9 | D$^{6/9}$/F$\sharp$

It felt good to be out of the rain.

| Em^9 | D$^{6/9}$/F$\sharp$

In the desert you can remember your name

| Em | D/F$\sharp$ D/A

'Cause there ain't no-one for to give you no pain.

Link

| Em^9 | D$^{6/9}$/F$\sharp$ | Em^9 | D$^{6/9}$/F$\sharp$

La la,   la la la la la, la la la, la   la.

| Em^9 | D$^{6/9}$/F$\sharp$ | Em^9 | D/A

La la,   la la la la la, la la la, la   la.

Verse 2

| Em | D/F$\sharp$

After two days in the desert sun

| Em | D/F$\sharp$

My skin began to turn red.

| Em | D/F$\sharp$

After three days in the desert fun

| Em | D/A

I was looking at a river bed:

| Em | D/F$\sharp$

And the story it told of a river that flowed

| Em | D/F$\sharp$ D/A

Made me sad to think it was dead.

Chorus 2

| Em⁹ | D⁶/⁹/F♯

You see I've been through the desert on a horse with no name,

| Em⁹ | D⁶/⁹/F♯

It felt good to be out of the rain.

| Em⁹ | D⁶/⁹/F♯

In the desert you can remember your name

| Em | D/F♯   D/A

'Cause there ain't no-one for to give you no pain.

Link 2

| Em⁹ | D⁶/⁹/F♯ | Em⁹ | D⁶/⁹/F♯ Bm⁷

La la la,   la la la la la, la la la, la la.

| Em⁹ | D⁶/⁹/F♯ | Em⁹ | A

La la la,   la la la la la, la la la, la la.

Guitar solo

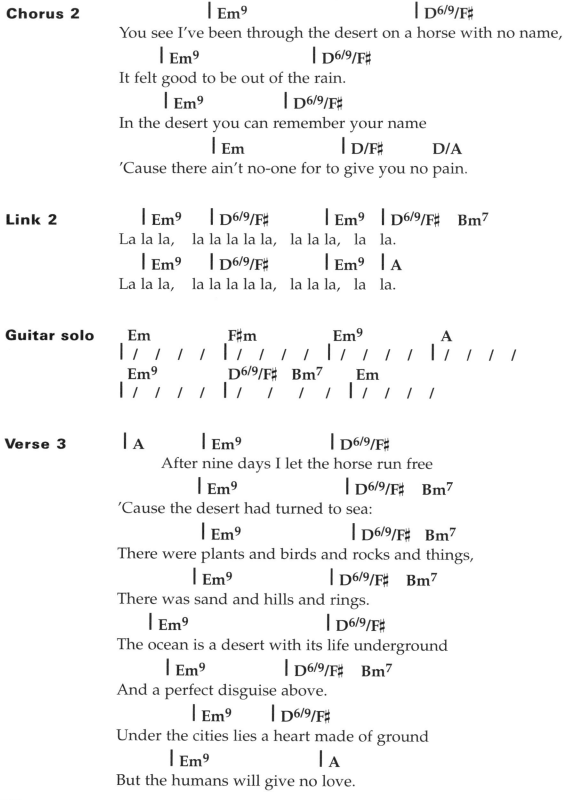

```
Em            F♯m          Em⁹              A
| / / / /  | / / / /  | / / / /  | / / / /
Em⁹           D⁶/⁹/F♯  Bm⁷     Em
| / / / /  | /  /  /  /  | / / / /
```


Verse 3

| A | Em⁹ | D⁶/⁹/F♯

After nine days I let the horse run free

| Em⁹ | D⁶/⁹/F♯ Bm⁷

'Cause the desert had turned to sea:

| Em⁹ | D⁶/⁹/F♯ Bm⁷

There were plants and birds and rocks and things,

| Em⁹ | D⁶/⁹/F♯ Bm⁷

There was sand and hills and rings.

| Em⁹ | D⁶/⁹/F♯

The ocean is a desert with its life underground

| Em⁹ | D⁶/⁹/F♯ Bm⁷

And a perfect disguise above.

| Em⁹ | D⁶/⁹/F♯

Under the cities lies a heart made of ground

| Em⁹ | A

But the humans will give no love.

Chorus 3

| Em^9

You see I've been through the desert on a horse with no name,

| Em^9 | D$^{6/9}$/F♯

It felt good to be out of the rain.

| Em^9 | D$^{6/9}$/F♯

In the desert you can remember your name

| Em | D/F♯   D/A

'Cause there ain't no-one for to give you no pain.

Coda

| Em^9 | D$^{6/9}$/F♯ | Em^9 | D$^{6/9}$/F♯ Bm^7

La la la,   la la la la la, la la la, la la.

| Em^9 | D$^{6/9}$/F♯ | Em^9 | A

La la la,   la la la la la, la la la, la la.   *(repeat to fade)*

In The Summertime

Words and Music by
RAY DORSET

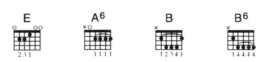

♩ = 80

Intro

```
       E                                    A⁶           E
4/4| /  /  /  / | /  /  /  / | /  /  /  / | /  /  /  /
       B    A⁶   E
   | /  /  /  / | /  /  /  / |
```

Verse 1

         E

In the summertime, when the weather is hot,

You can stretch right up and touch the sky.
         A⁶

When the weather's fine
                           E

You got women, you got women on your mind.
         B⁶

Have a drink, have a drive,
A⁶   E

Go out and see what you can find.

Verse 2
        E
If her daddy's rich take her out for a meal,

If her daddy's poor just do what you feel.
        A^6 E
Speed along the lane, do a ton or a ton-and-twenty-five.
        B^6
When the sun goes down
        A^6 E
You can make it, make it good in a lay-by.

Verse 3
        E
We're no threat, people, we're not dirty, we're not mean.

We love everybody but we do as we please.
        A^6
When the weather's fine
                       E
We go fishing or go swimming in the sea.
        B^6
We're always happy –
        A^6 E
Life's for living, yeah, that's our philosophy.

Chorus
        E
Sing along with us, dee dee dee-dee dee,

Dah dah dah-dah dah, yeah we're hap-happy.
A^6 E
Dah dah-dah, dee-dah-do dee-dah-do dah-do-dah.
        B^6 A^6 E
Dah-do-dah-dah-dah, dah-dah-dah do-dah-dah.

Alright-ah.

Instrumental

E A^6 E

| / / / / | / / / / | / / / / | / / / / |

B A^6 E

| / / / / | / / / / |

Verse 4

            E
When the winter's here, yeah it's party time,

Bring your bottle, wear your bright clothes,
                     A^6
It'll soon be summertime and we'll sing again –
                     E
We'll go driving or maybe we'll settle down.
   B^6
If she's rich, if she's nice,
       A^6 E
Bring your friends and we'll all go into town.

Instrumental

E A^6 E

| / / / / | / / / / | / / / / | / / / / |

B A^6 E

| / / / / | / / / / |

Verse 5

            E
In the summertime, when the weather is hot,

You can stretch right up and touch the sky.
       A^6
When the weather's fine
                              E
You got women, you got women on your mind.
      B^6
Have a drink, have a drive,
A^6 E
Go out and see what you can find.

Verse 6

        E
If her daddy's rich take her out for a meal,

If her daddy's poor just do what you feel.
      A⁶   E
Speed along the lane, do a ton or a ton-and-twenty-five.
      B⁶
When the sun goes down
      A⁶   E
You can make it, make it good in a lay-by.

Verse 7

        E
We're no threat, people, we're not dirty, we're not mean.

We love everybody but we do as we please.
      A⁶
When the weather's fine
                       E
We go fishing or go swimming in the sea.
      B⁶
We're always happy –
      A⁶   E
Life's for living, yeah, that's our philosophy.

Coda

      E
Sing along with us, dee dee dee-dee dee,

Dah dah dah-dah dah, yeah we're hap-happy.
A⁶   E
Dah dah-dah, dee-dah-do dee-dah-do dah-do-dah. *(fade)*

I Feel The Earth Move

Words and Music by
CAROLE KING

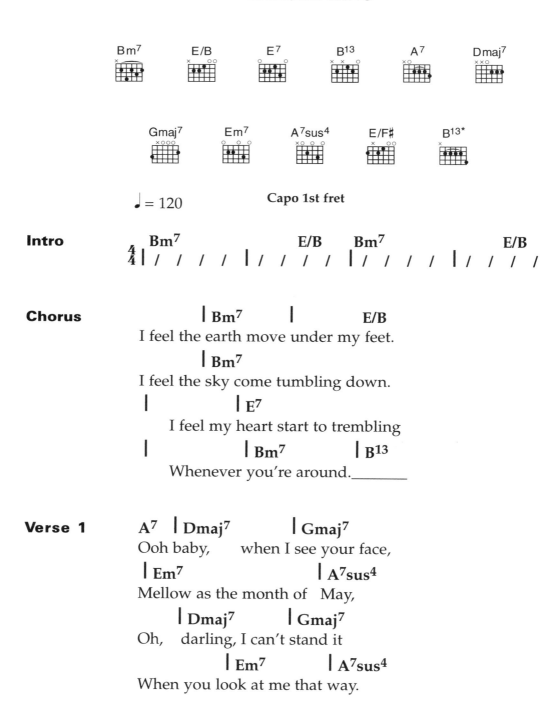

♩ = 120   Capo 1st fret

Intro
$\frac{4}{4}$ | Bm⁷ / / / / | / / / / | E/B / Bm⁷ / | E/B / / / |

Intro

| **Bm⁷** | | | **E/B** **Bm⁷** | | **E/B** |

$\frac{4}{4}$ | / / / / | / / / / | / / / / | / / / / |

Chorus

| **Bm⁷** | **E/B**
I feel the earth move under my feet.
| **Bm⁷**
I feel the sky come tumbling down.
| | **E⁷**
I feel my heart start to trembling
| | **Bm⁷** | **B¹³**
Whenever you're around._____

Verse 1

A⁷ | **Dmaj⁷** | **Gmaj⁷**
Ooh baby,   when I see your face,
| **Em⁷** | **A⁷sus⁴**
Mellow as the month of   May,
| **Dmaj⁷** | **Gmaj⁷**
Oh,   darling, I can't stand it
| **Em⁷** | **A⁷sus⁴**
When you look at me that way.

Chorus 2 E/F♯ | Bm⁷ | E/B
Hey, I feel the earth move under my feet.
          | Bm⁷
I feel the sky tumbling down.
     | | E⁷
     I feel my heart start to trembling
     | | Bm⁷ | B¹³ | Bm⁷ | B¹³ N.C.
     Whenever you're around._____ / / /

Instrumental   Bm⁷   E/B   Bm⁷   E⁷
          / / / / | / / / / | / / / / | / / / / :‖
     Bm⁷   E⁷   Bm⁷   E⁷
| / / / / | / / / / | / / / / | / / / /
     Bm⁷   E⁷   Bm⁷
| / / / / | / / / / | / / / /

Verse 2 | E⁷ A⁷ | Dmaj⁷ | Gmaj⁷
          Ooh darling,   when you're near me
          | Em⁷ | A⁷sus⁴
And you tenderly call my name,
     | Dmaj⁷ | Gmaj⁷
I know   that   my emotions
          | Em⁷ | A⁷sus⁴
Are something   I just can't tame.
          | E/F♯ | Bm⁷
I just got to have ya, baby.
     | E/B | Bm⁷ | E/B
     Uh, uh, uh,   uh, uh, uh,   yeah._____

Chorus 3

     Bm⁷ | E/B

I feel the earth move under my feet.

    | Bm⁷ | E/B   :‖

I feel the sky tumbling down, a-tumbling down.

     | Bm⁷ | E⁷

I just a-lose control _____

      | Bm⁷ | E⁷

Down to my very soul. _____

   | Bm⁷ | E⁷

I get hot and cold _____

   | Bm⁷ | E/B

All over, all over, all over, all over.

Chorus 4

     Bm⁷ | E/B

I feel the earth move under my feet.

    | Bm⁷

I feel the sky tumbling down,

    ⌐1   ⌐2

   | E/B

 a-tumbling down, a-tumbling down,

    | Bm⁷ | E/B

A-tumbling down, a-tumbling down,

      | Gmaj⁷ | B¹³*

A-tumbling down, tumbling down._____

Jealous Mind

Words and Music by
PETER SHELLEY

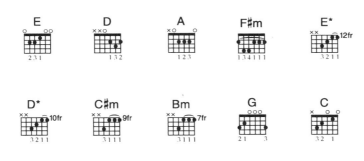

♩ = 136

horus

   A   **D**
Why is it I must know the things you're doing?
              A   **E**   **A**
Ah-ah-ah ah,____ it's just my jealous mind.

                               D
And when you're not at home I just can't take it,
              A   **E**   **A**
Ah-ah-ah ah,____ it's just my jealous mind.

erse 1

   E   **A**
I dread the time when you might leave me,
           F♯m   **E**
Deep in my heart a-don't ever go.
   E*   **D***   **C♯m Bm**
A-say you won't leave me.

Chorus 2   A   D

You could be out with him and I would   never know,

             A   E   A

Ah-ah-ah ah,____ it's just my jealous mind.

Instrumental A   G   A   C

‖: / / / / | / / / / | / / / / | / / / / :‖

Guitar link   E   D

| / / / / | / / / / | / / / / | / / / / |

Verse 2   E   A

I dread the time when you might leave me,

          F♯m   E

Deep in my heart,   a-don't ever go.

    E*   D*   C♯m Bm

A-say you won't leave me.

Chorus 3   A   D

Stay with me all the time, say there's no   other guy,

           A   E   A

Ah-ah-ah ah,____ it's just my jealous mind.

D   A   E   A

I love you so, it's just my jealous mind.

       D   E   A
Forgive my jealous mind,
      D   E   A
It's just my jealous mind,
          D   E   A
Blame it on my jealous mind,
         D   E   A
I can't help my jealous mind,
      D   E   A
It is just my jealous mind,
        D   E   A
It's in love that I'm so blind,
         D   E   A
Blame it on my jealous mind,
          D   E   A
Please forgive my jealous mind,
        D   E   A
Well it's just my jealous mind,
        D   E   A
Blame it on my jealous mind.   *(fade)*

Judy Teen

**Words and Music by
STEVE HARLEY**

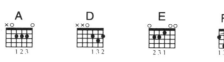

♩ = 126

Intro

(effects) A   D   A   D   E   A   N.C.
4/4 | / / / / | / / / / | / / / / | / / / ‖

Verse 1

A   D   A
Judy Teen,   the queen of the scene,
D E   A
She's rag doll amore.
         D   A
Verbal slanging, American twang,
D E   A
You dare not ignore.
       D A   D
In from New York, prompted her to talk
E   A
Of superballs.
      D A   D
Judy Teen grew sick of the scene,
   E   A
Just bragging to fools.

Chorus

E   F#m

She took us on a carousel,

     D   A

She made us smile and oh, how we laughed.

E   F#m

Together riding on a crest – it was swell,

     D   E

We stole her face and oh, how we laughed.

N.C.

She made us happy!

Link

A				D	A			D	E		A								

A D A D E A

| / / / / | / / / / | / / / / | / / / / |

Verse 2

A   D A   D

Sacral blues in various hues,

   E   A

She capered to draw me.

      D A   D

Me and yankie, all hanky panky,

E   A

Seldom she bored me.

       D   A   D

She's so bold and me feeling old,

   E   A

Just stroking her face.

      D A   D

Super trooper, he can show you

E   A

More than her lace.

Chorus 2

 E   F♯m
  She took us on a carousel,
     D   A
She made us smile and oh, how we laughed.
E   F♯m
  Together riding on a crest – it was swell,
     D   E
We stole her face and oh, how we laughed.
N.C.
She made us happy!

Instrumental

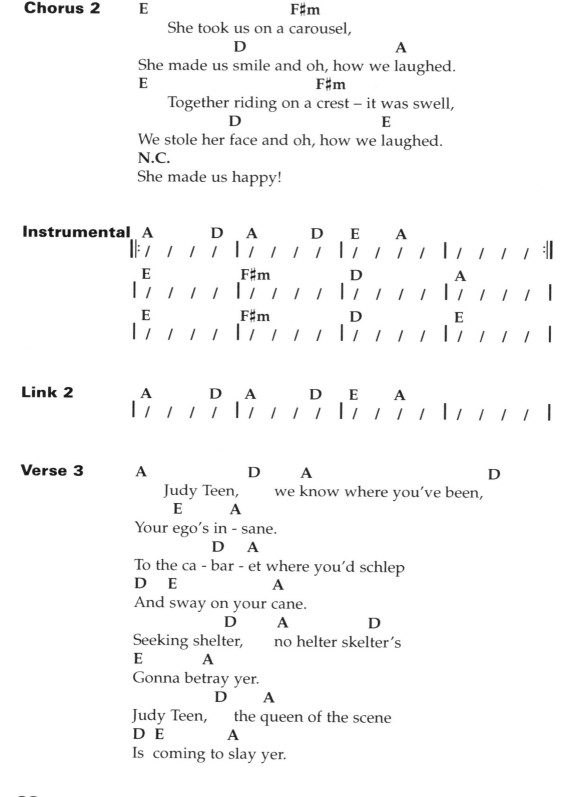

 A   D   A   D   E   A

 E   F♯m   D   A

 E   F♯m   D   E

Link 2

 A   D   A   D   E   A

Verse 3

 A   D   A   D
  Judy Teen,   we know where you've been,
  E   A
Your ego's in - sane.
       D   A
To the ca - bar - et where you'd schlep
D   E   A
And sway on your cane.
        D   A   D
Seeking shelter,   no helter skelter's
E   A
Gonna betray yer.
       D   A
Judy Teen,   the queen of the scene
D   E   A
Is coming to slay yer.

Chorus 3

   E   F♯m
     She took us on a carousel,
               D   A
She made us smile and oh, how we laughed.
E   F♯m
     Together riding on a crest – it was swell,
              D   E
We stole her face and oh, how we laughed.
N.C.
She made us happy!

Coda

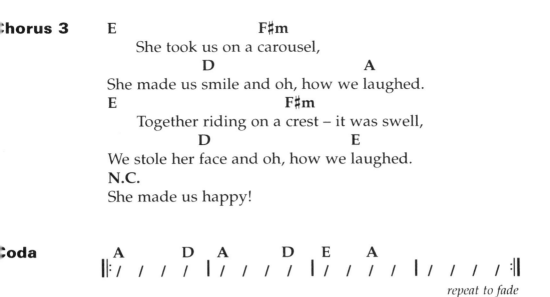

repeat to fade

Layla

Words and Music by
JIM GORDON AND ERIC CLAPTON

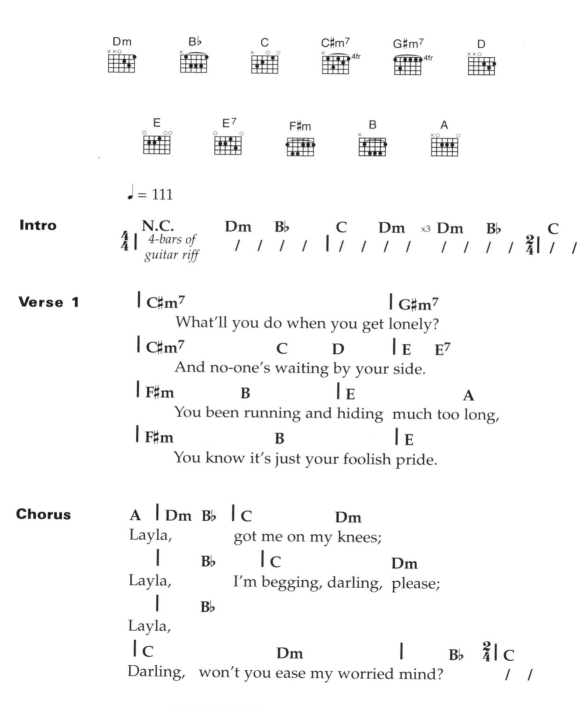

Verse 2

| C#m⁷ | G#m⁷

Tried to give you consolation

| C#m⁷   C   D | E   E⁷

When your old man had let you down.

| F#m   B | E   A

Like a fool, I fell in love with you,

| F#m   B | E

You turned my whole world upside down.

Chorus 2

A | Dm B♭ | C   Dm

Layla,   got me on my knees;

  | B♭ | C   Dm

Layla,   I'm begging, darling, please;

  | B♭

Layla,

| C   Dm | B♭   ²⁄₄| C

Darling,   won't you ease my worried mind?   /   /

Verse 3

| C#m⁷ | G#m⁷

Let's make the best of the situation

| C#m⁷   C   D | E   E⁷

Before I finally go insane.

| F#m   B | E   A

Please don't say we'll never find a way,

| F#m   B | E

Don't tell me all my love's in vain.

Chorus 3   A | Dm B♭ | C   Dm
Layla,   got me on my knees;

      | B♭ | C   Dm
Layla,   I'm begging, darling, please;

      | B♭
Layla,

| C   Dm | B♭ | C   Dm
Darling,   won't you ease my worried mind?

Chorus 4 | B♭ | C   Dm
Lay - la,   got me on my knees;

      | B♭ | C   Dm
Layla,   I'm begging, darling, please;

      | B♭
Layla,

| C   Dm | B♭ | C   Dm
Darling,   won't you ease my worried mind?

Coda   Dm   B♭   C   Dm
‖: / / / / | / / / / :‖   *to fade*

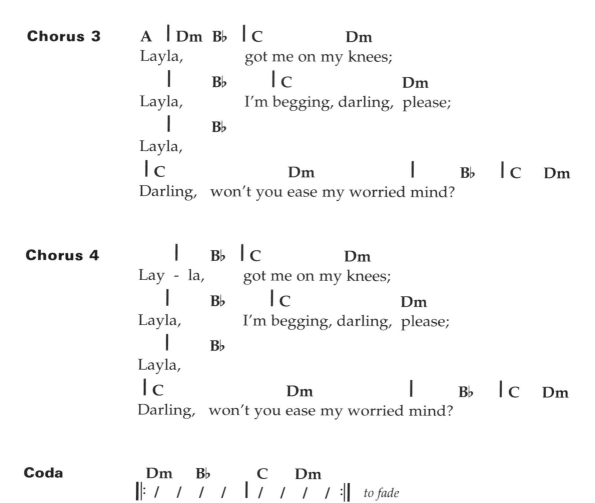

Livin' Thing

Words and Music by
JEFF LYNNE

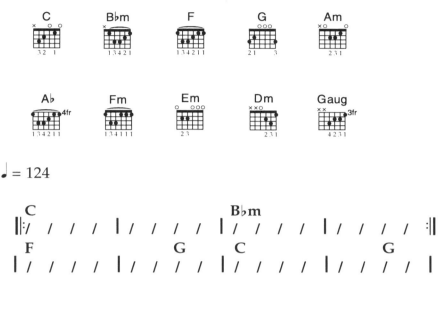

♩ = 124

Intro

```
        C                              Bbm
||: /  /  /  /  | /  /  /  /  | /  /  /  /  | /  /  /  / :||
F                    G     C                    G
| /  /  /  /  | /  /  /  /  | /  /  /  /  | /  /  /  / |
```

Verse 1

C
Sailing away on the crest of a wave –
    Am
It's like magic.
     Ab
Oh, rolling and riding and slipping and sliding –
  Fm
It's magic.
    Em   Dm
And you   and your sweet desire,
      Em Dm
You took me_____
    Em   F   G
Oh,   higher and higher, baby.

Chorus

```
C          Am
   It's a livin' thing,
F          Dm     Gaug   C
   It's a terrible thing to lose.
         Am
It's a given thing,
F          Dm     Gaug   C
   What a terrible thing to lose.
```

Link

```
  C                              Bbm
| (lose.)        | / / / / / | / / / / / | / / / / / |
  C                              Bbm                 G
| / / / / / | / / / / / | / / / / / | / / / / / |
  C                   G
| / / / / / | / / / / / |
```

Verse 2

```
C
Making believe this is what you conceived
            Am
From your worst day (I'm taking a dive).
       Ab
Oh,  moving in line, then you look back in time
          Fm
To the first day (I'm taking, I'm taking).
      Em                      Dm
And you    and your sweet desire,
                          Em  Dm
(Don't you do it) you took me_____
       Em              F      G
Oh,      higher and higher, baby.
```

Chorus 2

```
C          Am
   It's a livin' thing,
F          Dm     Gaug   C
   It's a terrible thing to lose.
         Am
It's a given thing,
F          Dm     Gaug   C
   What a terrible thing to lose.
```

Bridge

```
    C                              Bbm             F      G
  | (lose.)      | (I'm taking a dive,    on the slide,   hey!)
    C                      G
  | /  /  /  /  | /  /  /  /  |
```

Verse 3

C
Taking a dive 'cause you can't halt the slide
       Am
Floating downstream (I'm taking a dive)
      Ab
Oh, so let her go, don't start spoiling the show,
     Fm
It's a bad dream (I'm taking, I'm taking).
     Em   Dm
And you   and your sweet desire.
                       Em Dm
(Don't you do it) you took me_____
     Em   F   G
Oh,   higher and higher, baby.

Chorus 3

C   Am
  It's a livin' thing,
F   Dm   Gaug C
  It's a terrible thing to lose.
      Am
It's a given thing,
F   Dm   Gaug C
  What a terrible thing to lose.

Chorus 4

C   Am
  It's a livin' thing,
F   Dm   Gaug C
  It's a terrible thing to lose.
      Am
It's a given thing, *(fade)*

Life On Mars

Words and Music by
DAVID BOWIE

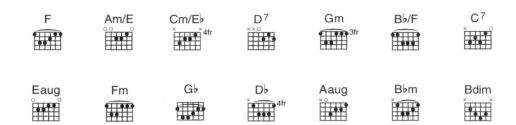

♩ = 57

Verse 1 ²₄ | F | Am/E | Cm/E♭
It's a god awful small affair
| D⁷
To the girl with the mousy hair
| Gm | B♭/F | C⁷
But her mummy is yelling 'No'
| | F
And her daddy has told her to go.
| Am/E | Cm/E♭
But her friend is nowhere to be seen,
| D⁷
Now she walks through her sunken dream
| Gm | B♭/F | C⁷
To the seat with the clearest view
|
And she's hooked to the silver screen.

Prechorus | E♭ | Eaug | Fm
But the film is a saddening bore
| G♭
For she's lived it ten times or more.
| D♭ | Aaug | B♭m
She could spit in the eyes of fools____
| Bdim
As they ask her to focus on:

Chorus | B♭ | E♭
Sailors fighting in the dance hall –
| Gm | F♯aug | F
Oh man! Look at those cavemen go.
| Fm | Cm⁷
It's the freakiest show.
| E♭m⁷ | B♭
Take a look at the Law-man
| E♭
Beating up the wrong guy.
| Gm | F♯aug | F
Oh man! Wonder if he'll ever know
| Fm | Cm⁷
He's in the best selling show?
| E♭m⁷ | Gm⁷ | F♯aug | B♭/F | Em⁷⁽♭⁵⁾ |
Is there life on Mars?_____

Link   F   F♯dim Gm   Ddim Am   B♭   B♭m
| / / | / / | / / | / / | / / | / / | / / |

Verse 2

| F | Am/E | Cm/E♭

It's on Amerika's tortured brow

            | D^7

That Mickey Mouse has grown up a cow.

| Gm | B♭/F | C^7

Now the workers have struck for fame

      |

'Cause Lennon's on sale again.

| F | Am/E | Cm/E♭

See the mice in their million hordes

       | D^7 | Gm

From Ibiza to the Norfolk Broads.

        | B♭/F | C^7

'Rule Britannia' is out of bounds

     |

To my mother, my dog, and clowns.

Prechorus 2

| E♭ | Eaug | Fm

But the film is a saddening bore

       | G♭

'Cause I wrote it ten times or more.

| D♭ | Aaug | B♭m

It's about to be writ again

       | Bdim

As I ask you to focus on:

Chorus 2

| B♭ | E♭

Sailors fighting in the dance hall –

| Gm | F♯aug | F

Oh man! Look at those cavemen go.

| Fm | Cm⁷

It's the freakiest show.

| E♭m⁷ | B♭

Take a look at the Law-man

| E♭

Beating up the wrong guy.

| Gm | F♯aug | F

Oh man! Wonder if he'll ever know

| Fm | Cm⁷

He's in the best selling show?

| E♭m⁷ | Gm⁷ | F♯aug | B♭/F | Em⁷⁽♭⁵⁾ |

Is there life on Mars?_____

Coda

```
    F        F♯dim  Gm      B♭/F     B♭
| /  /  | /  /  | /  /  | /  /  | /  /
    B♭       E♭      E♭m     B♭
| /  /  | /  /  | /  /  | /     ‖
```

103

Lola

Words and Music by
RAYMOND DAVIES

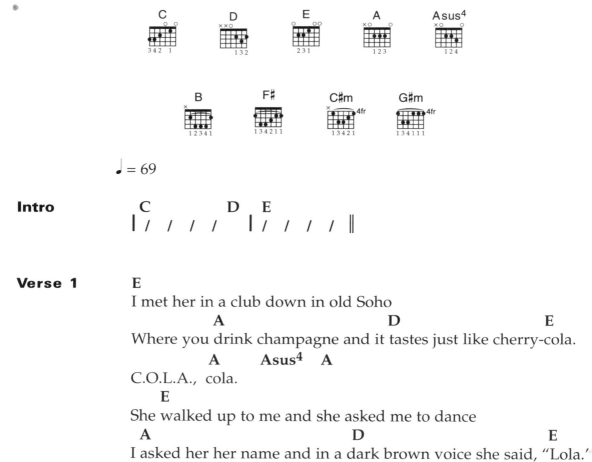

♩ = 69

Intro

| C | | | | | D | E | | | | | |

Verse 1

E
I met her in a club down in old Soho
          A   D   E
Where you drink champagne and it tastes just like cherry-cola.
          A   Asus⁴   A
C.O.L.A., cola.
    E
She walked up to me and she asked me to dance
  A   D   E
I asked her her name and in a dark brown voice she said, "Lola."
        A   D   C   D
L.O.L.A., Lola,   ler-ler-ler-ler-Lola.

Link 1

E
| / / / / / | / / / / / ||

Verse 2
       E
Well, I'm not the world's most physical guy
          A   D
But when she squeezed me tight she nearly broke my spine,
          E   A   Asus⁴ A
Oh my Lola, ler-ler-ler-ler-Lola.
        E
Well, I'm not dumb but I can't understand
       A   D
Why she walked like a woman but talked like a man,
        E   A D   C   D
Oh my Lola, ler-ler-ler-ler-Lola,   ler-ler-ler-ler-Lola.

Link 2
    E
| / / / / | / / / / ‖

Bridge
          B
Well, we drank champagne and danced all night
F♯
Under electric candlelight.
    A
She picked me up and sat me on her knee

And said, "Dear boy, won't you come home with me?"

Verse 3
         E
Well, I'm not the world's most passionate guy
          A   D   E
But when I looked in her eyes, well, I almost fell for my Lola,
           A D   C   D
Ler-ler-ler-ler-Lola,   ler-ler-ler-ler-Lola.

Chorus 1   E   A D   C   D
Lola, Ler-ler-ler-ler-Lola,   ler-ler-ler-ler-Lola.

Link 3

E

| / / / / | / / / / ‖

Bridge 2

   A   C♯m B A   C♯m B
I pushed her away, I walked to the door,
 A C♯m B   E   G♯m C♯m
I fell to the floor, I got down on my knees,
    B
Then I looked at her and she at me.

Verse 4

      E
Well, that's the way that I want it to stay,
    A   D   E
And I always want it to be that way for my Lola,
       A   Asus⁴ A
Ler-ler-ler-ler-Lola.
E
Girls will be boys and boys will be girls,
    A   D   E
It's a mixed-up, muddled-up, shook-up world except for Lola,
      A
Ler-ler-ler-ler-Lola.

Bridge 3

     B
Well, I left home just a week before
    F♯
And I'd never ever kissed a woman before,
    A
But Lola smiled and took me by the hand

And said, "Little boy, I'm gonna make you a man."

Verse 5

      E
Well, I'm not the world's most masculine man
    A   D
But I know what I am and I'm glad I'm a man,
        E   A D   C   D
And so is Lola, ler-ler-ler-ler-Lola, ler-ler-ler-ler-Lola.

Chorus 2

     E   A D   C   D
‖: Lola, ler-ler-ler-ler-Lola, ler-ler-ler-ler-Lola.   :‖ *repeat to fade*

Long Train Runnin'

Words and Music by
TOM JOHNSTON

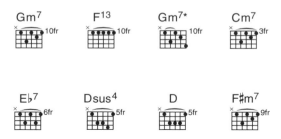

♩ = 115

Intro

Gm⁷ F¹³ Gm⁷ F¹³ ₓ₃ Gm⁷ F¹³ Gm⁷*
4/4 | / / / / | / / / / :|| / / / / | / / / /

Verse 1

| Gm⁷   F¹³
Down around the corner
| Gm⁷   F¹³
A half a mile from here
| Gm⁷
See them long trains run
F¹³ | Gm⁷
And you watch them disappear.

Chorus

F¹³ | Cm⁷
Without love
| | Gm⁷   F¹³
    Where would you be now?
| Gm⁷   F¹³ | E♭⁷ | Dsus⁴ D | Gm⁷   F¹³
Without love. _____

Verse 2

| Gm^7 F^{13} | Gm^7 F^{13}

      You know I saw Miss Lucy

| Gm^7 F^{13}

Down along the tracks.

   | Gm^7

She lost her home and her family

F^{13} | Gm^7

And she won't be coming back.

Chorus 2

F^{13} | Cm^7

Without love

  | | Gm^7 F^{13}

    Where would you be now?

| Gm^7 F^{13} | E♭^{7} | Dsus^4 D | Gm^7 F^{13}

    Without love. _____

Verse 3

| Gm^7 F^{13} | Gm^7 N.C.

    Well the Illinois Central

F♯m^7 | Gm^7 N.C.

And the Southern Central Freight

F♯m^7 | Gm^7 N.C.

Gotta keep   on pushing, mama,

Gm^7 |

'Cause you know they're runnin' late

Chorus 3

    | Cm^7

Without love

  | | Gm^7 F^{13}

    Where would you be now – now, now, now?

| Gm^7 F^{13} | E♭^{7} | Dsus^4 D | Gm^7 F^{13} | Gm^7 F^{13} |

    Without love. _____   / / / /

Harmonica solo

Gm⁷*

| / / / / | / / / / | / / / / | / / / / |

Cm⁷   Gm⁷*   F¹³ Gm⁷   F¹³

| / / / / | / / / / | / / / / | / / / / |

E♭⁷   Dsus⁴ D   Gm⁷   F¹³

| / / / / | / / / / | / / / / |

Verse 4

| Gm⁷ F¹³ | Gm⁷ N.C.

            Well the Illinois Central

F♯m⁷ | Gm⁷ N.C.

And the Southern Central Freight

F♯m⁷ | Gm⁷ N.C.

Gotta keep   on pushing, mama,

Gm⁷ |

'Cause you know they're runnin' late

Chorus 4

F¹³ | Cm⁷

Without love

| | Gm⁷   F¹³

     Where would you be now?

| Gm⁷ F¹³ | E♭⁷ | Dsus⁴ D | Gm⁷   F¹³

      Without love. _____

Verse 5

| Gm⁷ F¹³ | Gm⁷

            Well, pistons keep on churning

F♯m⁷ | Gm⁷

And the wheels go 'round and 'round,

F♯m⁷ | Gm⁷

And the steel rails are cold and hard

F♯m⁷ | Gm⁷   Gm⁷*

In the miles that they go down.

Chorus 5

| Cm⁷

Without love

| | Gm⁷   F¹³

    Where would you be right now?

| Gm⁷ F¹³ | E♭⁷ | Dsus⁴ D | Cm⁷

        Without love, _____ ooh.

(freely) |

Where would you be now?

Coda

   Gm⁷   F¹³ Gm⁷   F¹³ Gm⁷   F¹³ Gm⁷*

‖: / / / / | / / / / | / / / / | / / / / :‖

(with vocal ad lib.)   *repeat to fade*

Lust For Life

Words and Music by
DAVID BOWIE AND JAMES OSTERBERG

A	G	D	E7	G7	E

♩ = 100 (double time feel)

Intro

N.C.   (A)   A   G D x4
4/4 |drums 2-bars ‖: / / / / | / / / / :‖‖: / / / / :‖

E7   x4 A   G D x4 E7   x4
‖: / / / / :‖‖: / / / / :‖‖: / / / / :‖

G7   D
| / / / / | / / / / | / / / / | / / / /

E   A   G D A   G D
| / / / / | / / / / | / / / / | / / / /

Verse 1

|A   G D |A
Here comes   Johnny   Yen   again
G D |E7 |
    With the liquor and drugs   and the flesh machine.
| |
He's gonna do another strip-tease.
|A   G D |A   G D
Hey man, where'd you   get that   lotion?
|A   G   D |A
I've been hurting since I've   bought the gimmick
        |E7 |
About something called love, yeah, something called love.
    | |
Well, that's like hypnotizing chickens.

Chorus

| G⁷ |

Well, I'm just a modern guy.

| D |

Of course, I've had it in the ear before.

        | E |

I have a lust for life,

                | (A) | N.C. *drums*

'Cause   of a lust for life.   / / / /

Link

        (A)

| / / / / | / / / /

Verse 2

| |

I'm worth a million in prizes

            | (E⁷) |

With my torture film,   drive a GTO,

            | |

Wear a uniform   all on a government loan.

| A   G D | A

I'm worth a million   in prizes

G D | A   G D | A

  Yeah, I'm through with sleeping   on the sidewalk

      G D | E⁷ |

No more beating my brains, no more beating my brains

            | |

With liquor and drugs,   with liquor and drugs.

Chorus 2
| G⁷ |

Well, I'm just a modern guy

| D |

   Of course, I've had it in my ear before.

        | E |

Well, I've a lust for life (lust for life),

        | A |

'Cause of a lust for life (oooh),

       | |

I got a lust for life (oooh),

    | E⁷ | | |

Got a lust for life (oooh),   oh, a lust for life (oooh),

       | A   G D | A | G D | A

Oh, a lust for life   (oooh), a lust for life   (oooh),

     | E | | |

I got a lust for life (oooh), got a lust for life.   / / / /

Chorus 3
| G⁷ |

   Well, I'm just a modern guy.

| D |

   Of course, I've had it in the ear before.

    | E |

I have a lust for life,

      | A   G D | A

'Cause   of a lust for life.

Verse 3

G D | A   G D | A

Well, here comes Johnny   Yen again

| E⁷ |

With the liquor and drugs and the flesh machine.

| |

I know he's gonna do another strip-tease.

| A   G D | A

Hey man, where'd you   get that   lotion?

G D | A   G   D | A

Your skin starts itching once you   buy the gimmick

| E⁷ |

About something called love – oh love, love, love.

| |

Well, that's like hypnotizing chickens.

Chorus 4

| G⁷ |

Well,   I'm just a modern guy.

| D |

Of course, I've had it in the ear before.

| E |

And I've a lust for life   (lust for life)

| A   G D | A

'Cause I've a lust for life   (lust for life)

G D | A   G D | A

Got a lust for life,   yeah, a lust for life.

| E |

I got a lust for life,   oh a lust for life.

| |

Got a lust for life, yeah, a lust for life.

| A   G D | A   G D

I got a lust for life,   a lust for life,

| A   G D | A

Lust for life,   lust for life,

| E

Lust for life. *(fade)*

Lyin' Eyes

Words and Music by
DON HENLEY AND GLENN FREY

G   Gmaj^7 C   Am^7 D^7 C/G

D/F#   Em^7 Bm^7 G^9 A   Am

♩ = 130

Intro

G	Gmaj^7	C	
/ / / /	/ / / /	/ / / /	/ / / /

Am^7	D^7	G	
/ / / /	/ / / /	/ / / /	/ / / /

Verse 1

G   Gmaj^7 C
City girls just   seem to find out   early
Am^7 D^7
How to open doors with just a smile.____
    G   Gmaj^7 C
A rich old man and   she won't have to wor - ry:
       Am^7 C   G
She'll dress up all in lace and go in style.___

Verse 2

G   Gmaj^7 C
Late at night a   big old house gets lonely –
       Am^7 D^7
I guess every form of refuge has its price.
       G   Gmaj^7 C
And it breaks her heart to think her love is only
       Am^7 C   G   C D^7
Given to a man with hands as cold as ice.

Verse 3

          G   Gmaj7   C

So she tells him she must go out for the evening

    Am7   D7

To comfort an old friend who's feeling down.

      G   Gmaj7   C

But he knows where she's going as she's leaving:

      Am7   C   G   D7 G

She is headed for the cheating side of town.

Chorus

N.C.   G   C/G   G   C G

You can't hide_____   your lyin' eyes,

          D/F♯ Em7 Bm7   Am7 D7

And your   smile_____   is a thin disguise.

           G   G9   C   A

I thought by now_____   you'd realize_____

      Am   D7   G

There ain't no way to hide your lyin' eyes.

Link

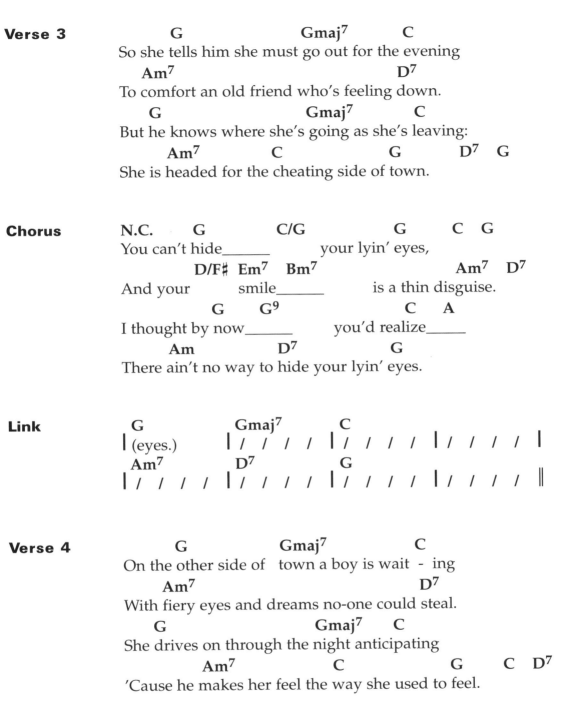

Verse 4

          G   Gmaj7   C

On the other side of   town a boy is wait - ing

     Am7   D7

With fiery eyes and dreams no-one could steal.

    G   Gmaj7   C

She drives on through the night anticipating

        Am7   C   G   C D7

'Cause he makes her feel the way she used to feel.

Verse 5

```
    G             Gmaj7         C
She rushes to his arms, they fall together;
    Am7                        D7
She whispers that it's only for awhile.
    G                            Gmaj7          C
She swears that soon she'll be coming back forever.
    Am7               C                        G        D7  G
She pulls away and leaves him with a smile.____
```

Chorus 2

```
N.C.        G          C/G              G        C   G
You can't hide______          your lyin' eyes,
            D/F♯ Em7   Bm7                  Am7   D7
And your         smile______      is a thin disguise.
               G     G9                  C     A
I thought by now______      you'd realize_____
      Am                D7               G
There ain't no way to hide your lyin' eyes.
```

Link

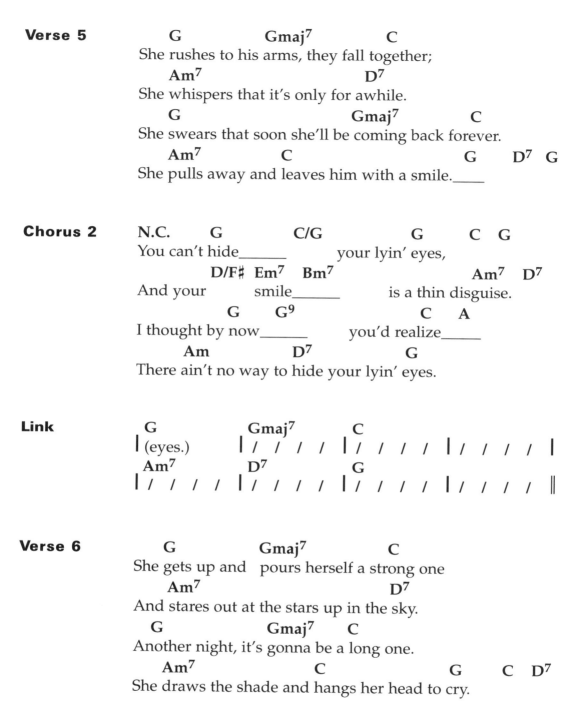

```
  G                Gmaj7          C
| (eyes.)        | / / / /      | / / / /      | / / / /      |
  Am7              D7             G
| / / / /        | / / / /      | / / / /      | / / / /      ||
```

Verse 6

```
    G              Gmaj7           C
She gets up and  pours herself a strong one
    Am7                             D7
And stares out at the stars up in the sky.
  G                Gmaj7     C
Another night, it's gonna be a long one.
    Am7                    C                G       C   D7
She draws the shade and hangs her head to cry.
```

Verse 7

G		Gmaj⁷		C

G   Gmaj⁷   C
She wonders how it ever got this crazy,
    Am⁷   D⁷
She thinks about a boy she knew in school.
      G   Gmaj⁷   C
Did she get tired or did she just get lazy?
      Am⁷   C   G
She's so far gone she feels just like a fool.

Verse 8

G   Gmaj⁷   C
My, oh my, you sure know how to arrange things –
    Am⁷   D⁷
You set it up so well, so carefully.
      G   Gmaj⁷   C
Ain't it funny how your new life didn't change things,
    Am⁷   C   G   D⁷   G
You're still the same old girl you used to be.____

Chorus 3

N.C.   G   C/G   G   C   G
You can't hide_____   your lyin' eyes,
      D/F♯   Em⁷   Bm⁷   Am⁷   D⁷
And your   smile_____   is a thin disguise.
      G   G⁹   C   A
I thought by now_____   you'd realize_____
    Am   D⁷   G   Gmaj⁷
There ain't no way to hide your lyin' eyes.

Coda

     Am   D⁷   G   Gmaj⁷
There ain't no way to hide your lyin' eyes.
Am   D⁷   G   Gmaj⁷
Honey, you can't hide your lyin' eyes.

(freely)

   Am   D⁷   G   C   G
| / / / / | / / / / | / / / | / ‖

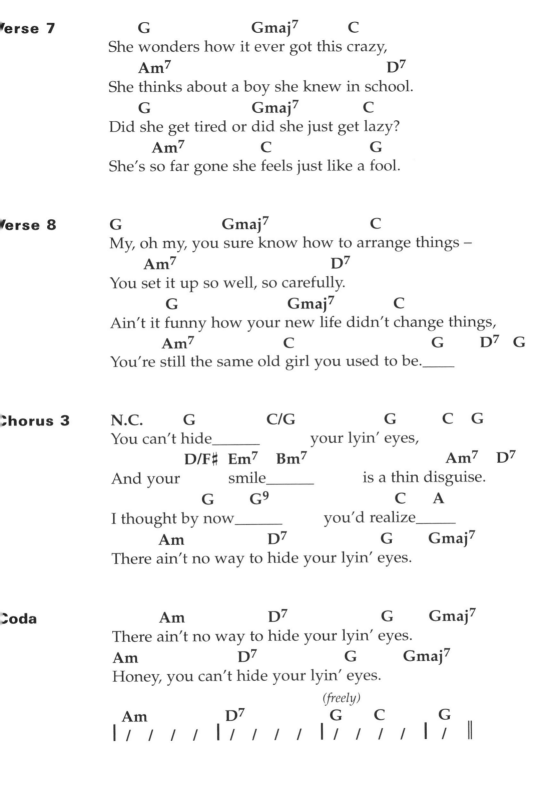

Maggie May

Words and Music by
ROD STEWART AND MARTIN QUITTENTON

[Chord diagrams: D, Em⁷, G, A, Em, F♯m⁷, Asus⁴, A⁷sus⁴]

♩ = 128

(half time feel)

Intro

$\frac{4}{4}$ | D / / / / | Em⁷ / / / / | G / / / / | D / G / / |

| D / / / / | Em⁷ / / / / | G / / / / | D / G / |

(a tempo)

Verse 1

| A | G | D

Wake up Maggie, I think I've got something to say to you:

| | A | G | D

It's late September and I really should be back at school.

| | G | D

I know I keep you amused

| G | A

But I feel I'm being used.

| Em | F♯m⁷ | Em

Oh Maggie, I couldn't have   tried any more.

| Asus⁴ | Em | A

You led me away from home

| Em | A

Just to save you from being alone.

| Em | A | D

You stole my heart and that's what really hurts.

Verse 2

| | | A | | G
The morning sun when it's in your face
| D
Really shows your age.
| | | A | | G
But that don't worry me none –
| D
In my eyes you're everything.
| | | G | | D
I laughed at all of your jokes,
| G | A
My love you didn't need to coax.
| Em | F♯m⁷ | Em
Oh Maggie, I couldn't have tried any more.
| Asus⁴ | Em | A
You led me away from home
| Em | A
Just to save you from being alone.
| Em | A | D
You stole my soul and that's a pain I can do without.

Verse 3

| | | A | | G | | D
All I needed was a friend to lend a guiding hand
| | | A
But you turned into a lover and,
| G | D
Mother, what a lover, you wore me out.
| | | G | | D
All you did was wreck my bed
| G | A
And in the morning kick me in the head.

| Em | F$\sharp$m^7 | Em

|Em |F♯m⁷ |Em

Oh Maggie, I couldn't have tried any more.

| Asus^4 | Em | A

You led me away from home

| Em | A

'Cause you didn't want to be alone.

| Em | A   G |D |

You stole my heart, I couldn't leave you if I tried.   / / / /

Instrumental   Em^7 A   D   G

| / / / / | / / / / | / / / / | / / / /

Em^7 D   G   A^{7}sus^4 D

| / / / / | / / / / | / / / / | / / / /

Verse 4 |A |G |D

I suppose I could collect my books and get on back to school,

| |A |G

Or steal my Daddy's cue

|D

And make a living out of playing pool,

| |G |D

Or find myself a rock and roll band

|G |A

That needs a helping hand.

| Em | F$\sharp$m^7 | Em

Oh Maggie,   I wished I'd never seen your face.

| Asus^4 | Em | A

You made a first class fool out of me

| Em | A

But I'm as blind as a fool can be.

| Em | A   G |D |

You stole my heart but I love you anyway.   / / / /

Instrumental

Em⁷   A   D   G
| / / / / | / / / / | / / / / | / / / / |

Em⁷   A   D
| / / / / | / / / / | / / / / | / / / / |

Em⁷   A   D   G
| / / / / | / / / / | / / / / | / / / / |

Em⁷   G
| / / / / | / / / / |

(half time feel)

D   Em⁷   G   D   x5
||: / / / / | / / / / | / / / / | / / / / :||

(a tempo)

Coda

| D | Em⁷ | G | D
Maggie,   I wish I'd   never seen your face.

D   Em⁷   G
| / / / / | / / / / | / / / / |

| D | | Em⁷ | G | D
     I'll get on back home,   one of these days.

| D | Em⁷ | G | D
Ooh._____ / / / /   / / / /

D   Em7   G   D   *(fade)* ||
| / / / / | / / / / | / / / / | / / / / |

Maid In Heaven

Words and Music by
BILL NELSON

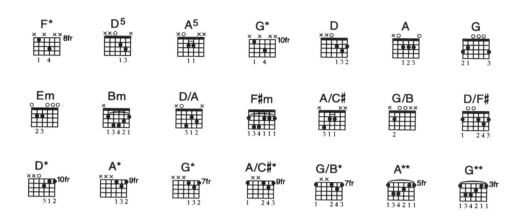

♩ = 132

Intro

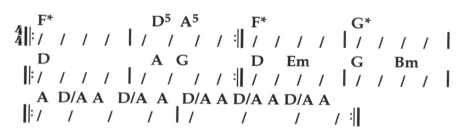

Verse 1

D   A G
She's a maid in Heaven,
Bm   F#m   Bm
He's a knight on the tiles,
A G   D   Em
A bat out of hell, oh well –
G   (D)
It's just a question of style.

ink
```
    D     A/C♯   G/B  G       D    A/C♯   G/B  G
 |(style.) /  /  | /  /  /  /  | /  /  /  /  | /  /  /  /  |
```

erse 2
```
    D              A    G
     It's a time    for giving
    Bm          F♯m          Bm
       In the two-star hotel
    A      G              D      Em
    Where breakfast in bed per head
    G                          (D)
        Is just the price of a smile.
```

ink 2
```
    D      A/C♯    G/B  G       D    A/C♯    G/B  G D/F♯
 |(smile.) /  /  | /  /  /  /  | /  /  /  /  | /  /  /  /  |
```

ridge
```
    Em  G  D
    I_____       know
    Em          G      D      F♯m
       It's not easy to live this way:
    Em          G              D      F♯m
       Just an hour and a fleeting kiss
              G      A
    'Til the morn - ing.
```

Link 3
```
       A    D/A A D/A  A     D/A A D/A A D/A A
 ‖:(-ing.)  /        /     / | /      /      / :‖
```

Verse 3
```
    D                 A  G
     Silent night of  wonders,
    Bm      F♯m                    Bm
       Day breaks through the door
    A  G              D      Em
    So broken and torn, reborn,
    G                              (D)
       Two shadows thrown on the floor.
```

Link 4

```
   D    A/C♯   G/B  G       D    A/C♯   G/B  G
| (floor.)  /   /  | /  /  /  / | /  /  /  / | /  /  /  / |
```

Verse 4

```
   D                   A    G
     Hold me now,    go lightly,
   Bm          F♯m          Bm
      Take the rough with the smooth –
   A  G        D        Em
   A  token of love, my love,
   G                           D     Em
      Was made in Heaven for you,
   G                           D     Em
      Was made in Heaven for you,
   G                           D     A/C♯ G/B A⁵ G D/F♯ Em
      Was made in Heaven for you._____
```

Link 5

```
   D
| /  /  /  /  / | /  /  /  /  / |
```

Coda

```
     D*                 A*  G*        x3
||: /  /  /  /  / | /  /  /  / :||
     D*               A/C♯*  G/B*  A**  G**  F♯m  Em  D
| /  /  /  /  / | /  /  /     /    | /  /    /     /  ||
```

Make Me Smile
(Come Up And See Me)

Words and Music by
STEVE HARLEY

G   F   C   Dm   Em   Am   G⁷

♩ = 136

Intro

$\frac{4}{4}$ (G)
| / / / / / | / / / / / | / / / / / | / / |

Verse 1

| N.C. | F | C | G
You've done it all: you've broken every code ____

| F | C | G⁷ |
And pulled the rebel to the floor.   / / / /

| G | F | C | G
You've spoilt the game, no matter what you say, ____

| F | C | G |
For only metal, what a bore._____

| F | C
Blue eyes,   blue eyes,

| F | C | G |
How can you tell so many lies?   / / / /

Chorus

| Dm | F | C | G
Come up and see me, make me smile._____

| Dm | F | C | G
I'll do what you want, running wild._____

Verse 2

| N.C. | | F | C | | G |

There's nothing left, all gone and run away.

| F | | C | G⁷ | |

Maybe you'll tarry for a while.   / / / /

| G | | F | C | | G |

It's just a test, a game for us to play.

| F | | C | | G | |

Win or lose, it's hard   to smile. _____

| F | | C |

Resist,   resist:

| F | | C | | G | |

It's from yourself you'll have to   hide. _____ / / / /

Chorus 2

| Dm | | F | | C | G |

Come up and see me, make me smile._____

| Dm | | F | | C | G |

I'll do what you want, running wild._____

Guitar solo

```
  N.C.        F          Em         F
| / / / / | / / / / | / / / / | / / / / |
  Am        Em                   G          G⁷
| / / / / | / / / / | / / / / | / / / / | / / / / |
  Dm        F          C          G
  / / / / | / / / / | / / / / | / / / / :‖
```


Verse 3

| N.C. | | F | C | | G |

There ain't no more: you've taken everything

| F | | C | G⁷ | |

From my belief in Mother Earth. / / / /

| G | | F | C | | G |

Can you ignore my faith in everything?

| F | | C | | G | |

'Cause I know what faith is and what it's   worth. _____

|F |C

Away, away,

|F |C |G |

And don't say   maybe you'll   try ___ / / / /

Chorus 3 |Dm |F |C |G

To come up and see me, to make me smile._____

|Dm |F |C |G |N.C.

I'll do what you want, just running wild._____

Link
   F   C   F   C

| / / / / / | / / / / / | / / / / / | / / / / /

   G

| / / / / / | / / / /

Chorus 4 |Dm |F |C |G

Come up and see me, make me smile._____

|Dm |F |C |G |N.C.

I'll do what you want, running wild._____

Link 2
   F   C   F   C

| / / / / / | / / / / / | / / / / / | / / / /

   G

| / / / / / | / / / /

to fade

Chorus 5 |Dm |F |C |G

Come up and see me, make me smile._____

|Dm |F |C |G

I'll do what you want, running wild._____

Mandolin Wind

Words and Music by
ROD STEWART

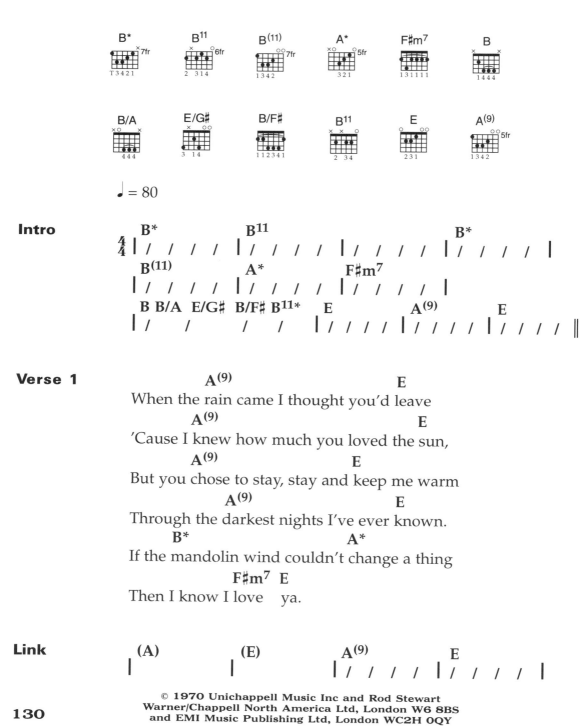

Intro

$\frac{4}{4}$

B* / / / / | B¹¹ / / / / | / / / / | B* / / / / |

B⁽¹¹⁾ / / / / | A* / / / / | F#m⁷ / / / / |

B B/A E/G# B/F# B¹¹* / / / / | E / / / / | A⁽⁹⁾ / / / / | E / / / / ‖

Verse 1

        A⁽⁹⁾   E
When the rain came I thought you'd leave
        A⁽⁹⁾   E
'Cause I knew how much you loved the sun,
        A⁽⁹⁾   E
But you chose to stay, stay and keep me warm
          A⁽⁹⁾   E
Through the darkest nights I've ever known.
        B*   A*
If the mandolin wind couldn't change a thing
          F#m⁷ E
Then I know I love   ya.

Link

(A) | (E) | A⁽⁹⁾ / / / / | E / / / / |

Verse 2

       A⁽⁹⁾   E
Oh the snow fell without a break:
A⁽⁹⁾   E
Buffalo died in the frozen fields you know
           A⁽⁹⁾   E
Through the coldest winter in almost fourteen years.
   A⁽⁹⁾   E
I couldn't believe you kept a smile.
        B*   A*
Now I can rest assured knowing that we've seen the worst
           F♯m⁷ E
And I know I love   ya.

Link

   (A)   (E)   A⁽⁹⁾   E
| | | / / / / | / / / / |

Verse 3

       A⁽⁹⁾   E
Oh, I never was good with romantic words
      A⁽⁹⁾   E
So the next few lines come really hard.
A⁽⁹⁾   E
Don't have much but what I've got is yours
    A⁽⁹⁾   E
Except, of course, my steel guitar.
        B*
Ha! 'cause I know you don't play
      A*
But I'll teach you one day
      F♯m⁷ E   (E⁷)
Because I love   ya.

Instrumental

  A⁽⁹⁾   E   x4 B*   A⁽⁹⁾
||: / / / / | / / / / :|| / / / / | / / / / |
  F♯m⁷   B⁽¹¹⁾   B*   A⁽⁹⁾
| / / / / | / / / / | / / / / | / / / / |
  F♯m⁷   B B/A E/G♯ B/F♯ B¹¹* E
| / / / / | /   /   /   / | / / / / ||

Link

A(9)   E

| / / / / / | / / / / / |

Verse 4

A(9)   E
I recall the night we knelt and prayed
A(9)   E
Noticing your face was thin and pale.
  A(9)   E
I found it hard to hide my tears.
  A(9)   E
I felt ashamed; I felt I'd let you down.
     B*   A*
No mandolin wind couldn't change a thing,
        F#m^7
Couldn't change a thing,
    B(11)
No, no.

Link
(with vocal ad lib.)

B*   A*   F#m^7 B(11)   x3

‖: / / / / / | / / / / / | / / / / / | / / / / / :‖

Coda

    B*   A*
The coldest winter in almost fourteen years
     F#m^7 B(11)   B*
Could never, never change your mind, yeah.
A*   F#m^7
  And I love ya,
           B(11)
Yes indeed and I love ya.
    B*
And I love ya,
      A*
Lordy, I love ya.
      F#m^7 B(11)
Ooh._____   *(fade)*

The Man Who Sold The World

Words and Music by
DAVID BOWIE

$\downarrow$ = 114

Intro

$\frac{4}{4}$ | A⁷ / / / / | / / / / | Dm / / / / | / / / / |

| F / / / / | / / / / |

Verse 1

Dm N.C.   A⁷
     We passed upon the stair, we spoke of was and when.
Dm   A⁷
     Although I wasn't there, he said I was his friend –
F   C   A⁷
     Which came as some surprise, I spoke into his eyes:
              Dm   C
"I thought you died alone a long, long time ago."

Chorus

       C   F
"Oh no, not me…
   D♭   F
I never lost control.
      C   F
You're face to face
        D♭   A⁷
With the man who sold the world."

Link

A⁷   Dm
| (world.") | / / / / / | / / / / / | / / / / / |
F
| / / / / / | / / / / / |

Verse 2

Dm N.C.   A⁷
    I laughed and shook his hand, and made my way back home
Dm   A⁷
   I searched for form and land, for years and years I roamed.
F   C   A⁷
   I gazed a gazely stare   at all the millions here.
                   Dm   C
We must have died alone a long, long time ago.

Chorus 2

       C   F
"Who knows? not me…
      D♭
We never lost control.
F   C   F
   You're face to face
       D♭   A⁷
With the man who sold the world."

Link 2

A⁷   Dm
| (world.") | / / / / / | / / / / / | / / / / / |
F   Dm
| / / / / / | / / / / / | / / / / / | / / / / / |

134

Chorus 3

      C   F
"Who knows? not me…
    D♭
We never lost control.
F   C   F
  You're face to face
      D♭   **A⁷**
With the man who sold the world."

Coda

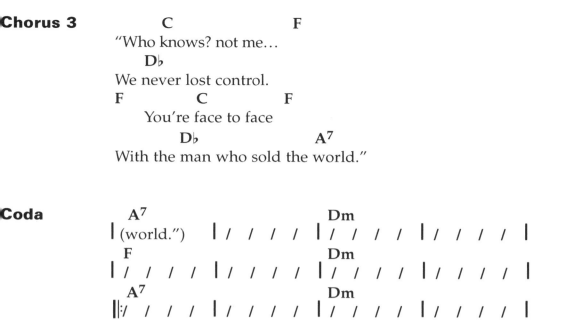

(repeat to fade)

Matchstalk Men And Matchstalk Cats And Dogs

Words and Music by
MICHAEL COLEMAN AND BRIAN BURKE

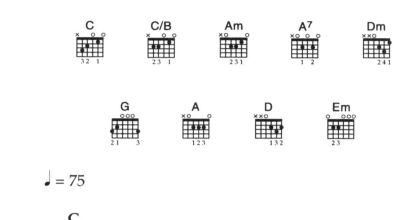

♩ = 75

Intro

(fade in) $\frac{4}{4}$ **C**
| / / / / / | / / / / / |

Verse 1

    C
He painted Salford's smokey tops
C/B Am
On cardboard boxes from the shop,
    A⁷   **Dm**
And parts of Ancoats where I used to play.

I'm sure he once walked down our street
              C
'Cause he painted kids who had nowt on their feet,
   G   **C**
The clothes we wore had all seen better days.

Link

    C   **Am**   **Dm** **G**
| (days.) / / | / / / / |

Verse 2

          C
Now they said his works of art were dull,
C/B Am
No room, all round   the walls are full,
    A^7 Dm
But Lowry didn't care much anyway.

They said, "He just paints cats and dogs
     C
And matchstalk men in boots and clogs."
    G   C
And Lowry said "That's just the way they'll stay."

Chorus

G   C   Dm
   And he painted matchstalk men and matchstalk cats and dogs,
        G
He painted kids on the corner of the street
        C
That were sparking clogs.

Now he takes his brush and he waits
    Dm
Outside them factory gates
        G   C
To paint his matchstalk men and matchstalk cats and dogs.

Verse 3

        C
Now canvas and brushes were wearing thin
C/B   Am
When London started calling him
    A^7 Dm
To come on down and wear the old flat cap.

They said, "Tell us all about your ways
      C
And all about them Salford days –
     G   C
Is it true you're just an ordinary chap?"

Chorus 2

    G   C   Dm

And he painted matchstalk men and matchstalk cats and dogs,

        G

He painted kids on the corner of the street

              C

That were sparking clogs.

Now he takes his brush and he waits

    Dm

Outside them factory gates

            G   C

To paint his matchstalk men and matchstalk cats and dogs.

Verse 4

          C

Now Lowrys hang upon the wall

C/B   Am

    Beside the greatest of them all,

    A⁷   Dm

And even the Mona Lisa takes a bow.

This tired old man with hair like snow

        C

Told Northern folk it's time to go;

    G   C

The fever came and the good Lord mopped his brow.

Chorus 3

    G   C   Dm

And he left us matchstalk men and matchstalk cats and dogs,

        G

He left us kids on the corner of the street

              C

That were sparking clogs.

Now he takes his brush and he waits

    Dm

Outside them pearly gates

            G   C

To paint his matchstalk men and matchstalk cats and dogs.

Chorus 4

       A   D   Em

‖: And he left us matchstalk men and matchstalk cats and dogs,

       A

He left us kids on the corner of the street

              D

That were sparking clogs.

Now he takes his brush and he waits

      Em

Outside them pearly gates

          A   D

To paint his matchstalk men and matchstalk cats and dogs. :‖

(repeat chorus to fade)

A Message To You Rudy

Words and Music by
ROBERT THOMPSON

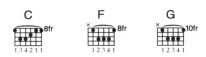

♩ = 98

Intro

(C)　　　　　　(F)　(G)　　　C　　　　　　　F　　G

4/4 ‖: / / / / | / / / / :‖| / / / / | / / / / :‖

Verse 1

C　　　　　　　　　　　　　　F　G
Stop your messing around (ah-ah-ah),
C　　　　　　　　　　　　　　F　G
Better think of your future (ah-ah-ah).
C　　　　　　　　　　　　　　F
Time you straighten right out (ah-ah)
　　　　　　　　G　　　　　C　　　F　G
Creating problems in town (ah-ah-ah).

Chorus

　　　C　　F　　　　G
Rudy, a message to you,
　　　C　　F　　　　G
Rudy, a message to you.

Link

　　C　　　　　　　F　　G　　　C　　　　　　　F　　G
| / / / / | / / / / | / / / / | / / / / |

Verse 2

```
C                                F  G
Stop your fooling around (ah-ah-ah),
C                                F  G
Time you straighten right out (ah-ah-ah).
C                              F
Better think of your future (ah-ah)
             G          C     F  G
Else you'll wind up in jail (ah-ah-ah).
```

Chorus 2

```
   C    F       G
Rudy, a message to you,
   C    F        G
Rudy, a message to you.
```

Link 2

```
C               F   G    C               F   G
| / / / / | / / / / | / / / / | / / / / |
```

Brass solo

```
C               F   G    C               F   G
||: / / / / | / / / / | / / / / | / / / / :||
```

Verse 3

```
C                              F  G
Stop your messing around (ah-ah-ah),
C                              F  G
Better think of your future (ah-ah-ah).
C                                F
Time you straighten right out (ah-ah)
             G          C     F  G
Creating problems in town (ah-ah-ah).
```

Chorus 3

```
   C    F       G
Rudy, a message to you,
   C    F       G
Rudy, a message to you.
```

Coda

```
      C       F       G
||: Rudy, it's a message to you. :|| repeat to fade, (vocal ad lib.)
```

141

Miss You

Words and Music by
MICK JAGGER AND KEITH RICHARDS

Am Dm7 Am* Dm7*

F Em Dm E

♩ = 105

Intro   4/4   **Am**   **Dm7**
| / / / / | / / / / | / / / / | / / / / |
Am   **Dm7**
| / / / / | / / / / | / / / / |

Verse 1 | | **Am** |
I've been holding out so long, I've been sleeping all alone,
        | **Dm7**
Lord I miss you.
        | | **Am** |
I've been hanging on the phone, I've been sleeping all alone,
        | **Dm7**
I want to kiss you.

Chorus 1   ‖: | **Am***
Oooh oooh oooh oooh oooh oooh oooh,
        |
Oooh oooh oooh oooh oooh oooh oooh,
        | **Dm7***   :‖
Oooh oooh oooh.

142

Verse 2

| | **Am**

Well, I've been haunted in my sleep, you've been

|

starring in my dreams,

    | **Dm7**

Lord I miss you child. | | **Am**

|

I've been waiting in the hall, been waiting on your call

    | **Dm7**

When the phone rings.

|

It's just a friend of mine that say,

    | **Am**

"Hey, what's the matter man?

|

We're gonna come round at twelve

      | **Dm7** |

With some Puerto Rican girls that are just dying to meet you.

    | **Am**

We're gonna bring a case of wine

|

Hey, let's go mess and fool around,

    | **Dm7**

You know, like we used to."

Chorus 2

‖: | **Am***

Aaah aaah aaah aaah aaah aaah aaah,

|

Aaah aaah aaah aaah aaah aaah aaah,

    | **Dm7***   :‖

Aaah aaah aaah-aaah.   / / / /

Bridge

| F | Em | Dm |
Oh, baby why you wait so long? / / / /
| F | Em | Dm |
Oh, baby why you wait so long?
| E
Won't you come home, come home!
| | Dsus2 A | Dsus2 A | E
I said, can't you see that this old boy has been a-lonely?

Link

| Am | | Dm7 |
/ / / / / / / / / / / /

Verse 3

| | Am |
(*spoken*) I've been walking in Central Park, singing after dark,
| Dm7
People think I'm crazy,
| | Am |
I've been stumbling on my feet, shuffling through the street,
| Dm7 |
Asking people, "What's the matter with you, boy?"
| Am | | Dm7 |
Sometimes I want to say to myself, sometimes I say:

Chorus 3

| Am*
Oooh oooh oooh oooh oooh oooh,
|
Oooh oooh oooh oooh oooh oooh oooh,
| Dm7*
I wanna kiss you, child.
| | Am7*
I guess I'm lying to myself:
|
It's just you and no-one else.

|Dm7*

Lord I wanna kiss you, child.

Chorus 4   ‖: |Am*

Ah ah ah ah ah ah ah,

|

Ah ah ah ah ah ah ah,

|Dm7*   :‖ *repeat vocal ad lib to fade*

Ah ah ah ah.

Moondance

Words and Music by
VAN MORRISON

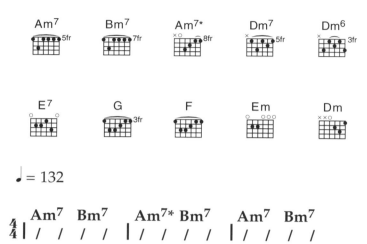

♩ = 132

Intro

$\frac{4}{4}$ | Am⁷ Bm⁷ / / / | Am⁷* Bm⁷ / / / | Am⁷ Bm⁷ / / /

Verse 1

| Am⁷* Bm⁷ | Am⁷ Bm⁷ | Am⁷*
    Well, it's a marvellous night for a Moondance

Bm⁷ | Am⁷ Bm⁷ | Am⁷*
    With the stars up above in your eyes,

Bm⁷ | Am⁷ Bm⁷ | Am⁷*
    A fantabulous night to make romance

Bm⁷ | Am⁷ Bm⁷ | Am⁷*
'Neath the cover of October skies.

Bm⁷ | Am⁷ Bm⁷ | Am⁷*
    And all the leaves on the trees are falling

Bm⁷ | Am⁷ Bm⁷ | Am⁷*
To the sound of the breezes that blow,

Bm⁷ | Am⁷ Bm⁷ | Am⁷*
    And I'm trying to please to the calling

Bm⁷ | Am⁷ Bm⁷ | Am⁷*
    Of your heart-strings that   play soft and low.

Bridge

Bm⁷ | Dm⁷ | Am⁷ | Dm⁷ | Am⁷

And all the night's magic seems to whisper and hush,

| Dm⁷ | Am⁷ | N.C. Dm⁶

And all the soft moonlight seems to shine

| N.C. E⁷

In your blush.

Chorus

| Am⁷ Dm⁷ | Am⁷ Dm⁷

Can I just have one a-more moondance

| Am⁷ Dm⁷ | Am⁷ Dm⁷

With you, my love?

| Am⁷ Dm⁷ | Am⁷ Dm⁷

Can I just make some more romance

| Am⁷ Dm⁷ | Am⁷ E⁷

With a-you, my love?

Verse 2

| Am⁷ Bm⁷ | Am⁷*

Well, I wanna make love to you tonight,

Bm⁷ | Am⁷ Bm⁷ | Am⁷*

I can't wait 'til the morning has come,

Bm⁷ | Am⁷ Bm⁷ | Am⁷*

And I know now the time is just right

Bm⁷ | Am⁷ Bm⁷ | Am⁷*

And straight into my arms you will run.

Bm⁷ | Am⁷ Bm⁷ | Am⁷*

And when you come my heart will be waiting

Bm⁷ | Am⁷ Bm⁷ | Am⁷*

To make sure that you're never alone,

Bm⁷ | Am⁷ Bm⁷ | Am⁷*

There and then all my dreams will come true, dear;

Bm⁷ | Am⁷ Bm⁷ | Am⁷*

There and then I will make you my own.

Bridge 2

Bm⁷ | Dm⁷ | Am⁷ | Dm⁷ | Am⁷

Bm^7 | Dm^7 | Am^7 | Dm^7 | Am^7

And every time   I touch you,   you just tremble inside,

| Dm^7 | Am^7 | N.C. Dm^6

Then I know how   much you want me that

N.C. | E^7

You can't hide.

Chorus 2

| Am^7 Dm^7 | Am^7 Dm^7

Can I just   have one a-more moondance

| Am^7 Dm^7 | Am^7 Dm^7

With you,   my love?

| Am^7 Dm^7 | Am^7 Dm^7

Can I just   make some more romance

| Am^7 Dm^7 | Am^7 E^7

With a-you,   my love?

Piano solo

Am^7 Bm^7 Am^{7*} Bm^7 x8

‖: / / / / | / / / / :‖

Sax solo

Dm^7 Am^7 Dm^7 Am^7

| / / / / | / / / / | / / / / | / / / /

Dm^7 Am^7 N.C. Dm^6 N.C. E^7

| / / / / | / / / / | / / / / | / / / /

$Am7$ Dm^7 Am^7 Dm^7 $Am7$ Dm^7 Am^7 Dm^7

| / / / / | / / / / | / / / / | / / / /

$Am7$ Dm^7 Am^7 Dm^7 $Am7$ Dm^7 Am^7 E^7

| / / / / | / / / / | / / / / | / / / Well it's a

Verse 3
(with vocal ad lib.)

| Am⁷   Bm⁷ | Am⁷*
Marvellous night for a Moondance

Bm⁷ | Am⁷   Bm⁷ | Am⁷*
   With the stars up above in your eyes,

Bm⁷ | Am⁷   Bm⁷ | Am⁷*
   A fantabulous night to make romance

Bm⁷ | Am⁷   Bm⁷ | Am⁷*
'Neath the cover of October skies.

Bm⁷ | Am⁷   Bm⁷ | Am⁷*
   And all the leaves on the trees are falling

Bm⁷ | Am⁷   Bm⁷ | Am⁷*
To the sound of the breezes that blow,

Bm⁷ | Am⁷   Bm⁷ | Am⁷*
   And I'm trying to please to the calling

Bm⁷ | Am⁷   Bm⁷ | Am⁷*
   Of your heart-strings that   play soft and low.

Bridge 3

Bm⁷ | Dm⁷ | Am⁷ | Dm⁷ | Am⁷
   And all the night's magic seems to whisper and hush,

    | Dm⁷ | Am⁷ | N.C.   Dm⁶
And all the soft   moonlight seems to shine

   | N.C.   E⁷
In your blush.

Chorus 3

  | Am⁷ Dm⁷ | Am⁷   Dm⁷
Can I just   have one a-more moondance

   | Am⁷ Dm⁷ | Am⁷   Dm⁷
With you,   my love?

   | Am⁷ Dm⁷ | Am⁷ Dm⁷
Can I just   make some more romance

   | Am⁷ Dm⁷ | Am⁷
With a-you,   my love?

149

Coda

E^7 | Am^7 Bm^7 | Am^{7*}

One more moondance with you

Bm^7 | Am^7 Bm^7 | Am^{7*} Bm^7

In the moonlight

| Am^7 Bm^7 | Am^{7*} Bm^7

On a magic night.

| Am^7 Bm^7 | Am^{7*} Bm^7 | Am^7 Bm^7 | Am^{7*} Bm^7

La,   la, la, la,   la   in the moonlight _____

| Am^7 Bm^7 | Am^{7*} Bm^7

On a magic   night.

| Am^7 G | F   Em | Dm N.C. | Am^7 ‖

Can't I just have one more dance with you, my love?

More Than A Feeling

Words and Music by
TOM SCHOLZ

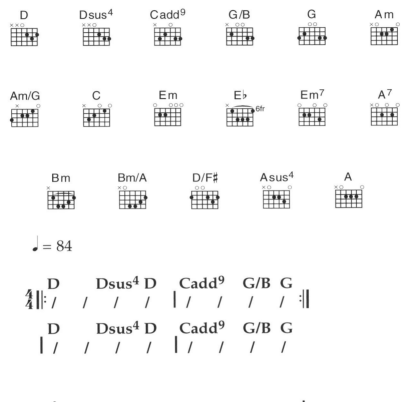

♩ = 84

Intro

```
        D        Dsus⁴ D   Cadd⁹   G/B G
  4 ‖: /   /   /   /  | /   /   /   /  :‖
  4
        D        Dsus⁴ D   Cadd⁹   G/B G
      | /   /   /   /  | /   /   /   /
```

Verse 1

      | D   Dsus⁴ D | Cadd⁹ G/B   G
I looked out this morn - ing and the sun was   gone,

      | D   Dsus⁴ D | Cadd⁹ G/B G
Turned on some mus - ic to start my day

          | D   Dsus⁴ D | Cadd⁹   G/B G
And lost myself   in a familiar song:

       | D   Dsus⁴ D | Cadd⁹ | G/B
I closed my eyes   and I slipped away._____

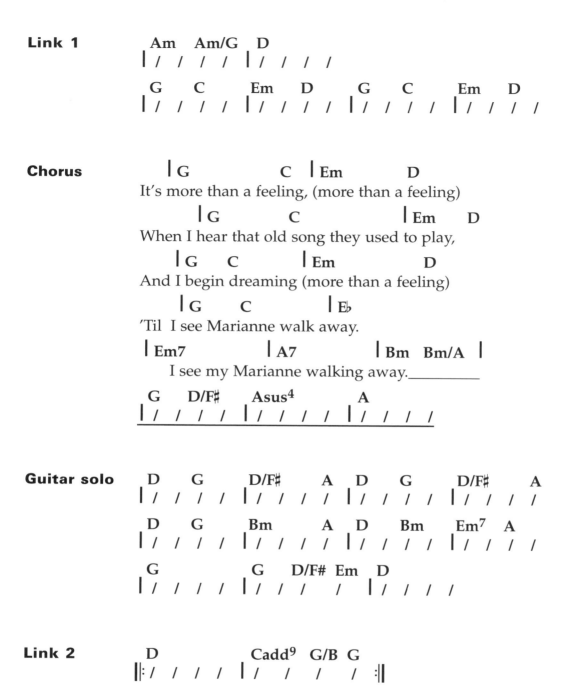

Link 1

Am Am/G D
| / / / / | / / / / |

G   C   Em   D   G   C   Em   D
| / / / / | / / / / | / / / / | / / / / |

Chorus

| G   C | Em   D
It's more than a feeling, (more than a feeling)

| G   C | Em   D
When I hear that old song they used to play,

| G C | Em   D
And I begin dreaming (more than a feeling)

| G   C | E♭
'Til I see Marianne walk away.

| Em7 | A7 | Bm Bm/A |
I see my Marianne walking away._____

G   D/F♯   Asus⁴   A
| / / / / | / / / / | / / / / |

Guitar solo

D   G   D/F♯   A D   G   D/F♯   A
| / / / / | / / / / | / / / / | / / / / |

D   G   Bm   A D   Bm   Em⁷ A
| / / / / | / / / / | / / / / | / / / / |

G   G   D/F# Em D
| / / / / | / / / / | / / / / |

Link 2

D   Cadd⁹ G/B G
||: / / / / | / / / / :||

152

Verse 2

| D   Dsus⁴ D | Cadd⁹   G/B   G

When I'm tir - ed and thinking cold

| D   Dsus⁴ D | Cadd⁹ G/B   G

I hide in my mu - sic, forget the day,

| D   Dsus⁴ D | Cadd⁹   G/B   G

And dream of a girl   I used to know

| D   Dsus⁴ D | Cadd⁹   G/B   Cadd⁹ |

I closed my eyes   and she slipped away._____

D   Dsus⁴ D   Cadd⁹   G/B   G   D   Dsus⁴ D
| /   /   /   /   / | /   /   /   / | /   /   /   /

| Cadd⁹   G/B   G | D   Dsus⁴ D | Cadd⁹   G/B   Cadd⁹

She slipped a-way._____

D   Dsus⁴ D   Cadd⁹   G/B
| /   /   /   /   / | /   /   /   / | /   /   /   /

Link 3

Am   Am/G   D
| /   /   /   /   / | /   /   /   / | /   /   /

G   C   Em   D   G   C   Em   D
| /   /   /   /   / | /   /   /   / | /   /   /   / | /   /   /   /

Chorus 2

| G   C | Em   D

It's more than a feeling, (more than a feeling)

| G   C | Em   D

When I hear that old song they used to play,

| G   C | Em   D

And I begin dreaming (more than a feeling)

| G   C | Em   D

'Til I see Marianne walk away._____

Coda

G   C   Em   D
||: /   /   /   / | /   /   /   /   :|| *to fade*

My Sweet Lord

Words and Music by
GEORGE HARRISON

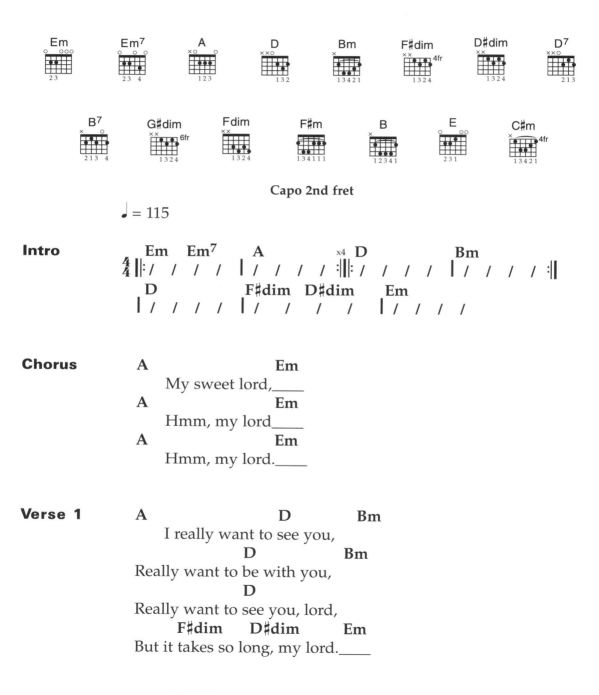

Capo 2nd fret

♩ = 115

Intro

| Em | Em⁷ | A | x4 D | Bm |

D   F♯dim D♯dim   Em

Chorus

A   Em
My sweet lord,____
A   Em
Hmm, my lord____
A   Em
Hmm, my lord.____

Verse 1

A   D   Bm
I really want to see you,
          D   Bm
Really want to be with you,
          D
Really want to see you, lord,
    F♯dim   D♯dim   Em
But it takes so long, my lord.____

Chorus 2

    A   Em
      My sweet lord,____
    A   Em
      Hmm, my lord____
    A   Em
      Hmm, my lord.____

Verse 2

    A   D   Bm
      I really want to know you,
                 D   Bm
    Really want to go with you,
                 D
    Really want to show you, lord,
      F♯dim   D♯dim   Em
    But it won't take long, my lord.____

Chorus 3

        A   Em
  (Hallelujah)   My sweet lord,____
        A   Em
  (Hallelujah)   Hmm my lord,____
        A   Em
  (Hallelujah)   My sweet lord.____
        A
  (Hallelujah).

Bridge

              D
    Really want to see you,
              D⁷
    Really want to see you,
              B⁷
    Really want to see you, lord;
              E
    Really want to see you, lord,
      G♯dim   Fdim F♯m
    But it takes so long, my   lord.

Chorus 4

     B   F♯m
(Hallelujah) My sweet lord,____
     B   F♯m
(Hallelujah) Hmm my lord,____
     B   F♯m
(Hallelujah) My my my lord.____
     B
(Hallelujah).

Verse 3

       E   C♯m
I really want to know you (hallelujah),
       E   C♯m
Really want to go with you (hallelujah),
       E
Really want to show you, lord,
   G♯dim   Fdim F♯m
But it won't take long, my lord.

Chorus 5

     B   F♯m
(Hallelujah) Hmm-hm-hm,
     B   F♯m
(Hallelujah) My sweet lord,
     B   F♯m
(Hallelujah) My, my lord.____
     B
(Hallelujah).

Guitar solo

```
  E              C♯m            E              C♯m
| / / / / / | / / / / / | / / / / / | / / / / / |
  E              G♯dim   Fdim
| / / / / / | / /  /  /  / |
```

Chorus 4

```
       F♯m    B              F♯m         B
    Hmm, my lord         (hare Krishna)
              F♯m            B
My, my, my lord (hare Krishna)
           F♯m                 B
Oh, my sweet lord (Krishna Krishna)
          F♯m          B
Ooh_____ (hare hare).
```

Verse 5

```
                         E              C♯m
   Now I really want to see you (hare rama)
                      E              C♯m
Really want to be with you (hare rama)
                   E
Really want to see you, lord,
       G♯dim    Fdim   F♯m
But it takes so long, my      lord.
       B                F♯m          B
(Hallelujah) my lord._____ (Hallelujah)
         F♯m           B
My, my, my lord (hare Krishna),
         F♯m          B
My sweet lord (hare Krishna),
              F♯m                B
My sweet lord      (Krishna Krishna),
        F♯m         B
My lord       (hare hare),
            F♯m           B
Hmm_____         (Gurur Brahma),
            F♯m            B
Hmm_____         (Gurur Vishnu),
          F♯m            B
Hmm_____         (Gurur Devo),
         F♯m            B
Hmm_____         (Maheshwara),
```

       F♯m   **B**
My sweet lord (Gurur Sakshaat),
         F♯m   **B**
My sweet lord (Parabrahma),
            F♯m   **B**
My, my, my lord (Tasmai Shree),
               F♯m   **B**
My, my, my, my lord (Guruve Namah),
         F♯m   **B**
My sweet lord (hare rama),
F♯m   **B**
   (hare Krishna),
             F♯m   **B**
My sweet lord (hare Krishna),
              F♯m   **B**
My sweet lord   (Krishna Krishna)
        F♯m
My lord   (hare hare).   *(fade)*

Nothing Rhymed

Words and Music by
RAYMOND O'SULLIVAN

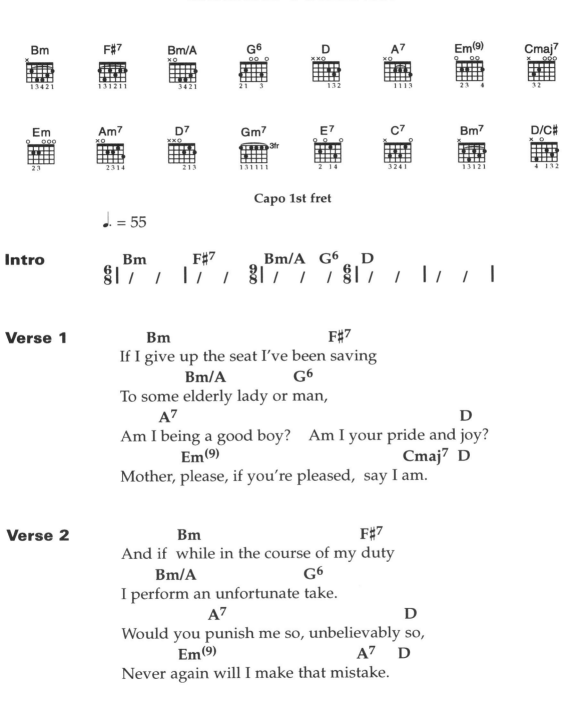

Capo 1st fret

$\stackrel{.}{\downarrow} = 55$

Intro

Bm   F#7   Bm/A G6   D

Verse 1

    Bm   F#7
If I give up the seat I've been saving
       Bm/A   G6
To some elderly lady or man,
     A7   D
Am I being a good boy?   Am I your pride and joy?
       Em(9)   Cmaj7 D
Mother, please, if you're pleased, say I am.

Verse 2

      Bm   F#7
And if while in the course of my duty
   Bm/A   G6
I perform an unfortunate take.
      A7   D
Would you punish me so, unbelievably so,
   Em(9)   A7   D
Never again will I make that mistake.

Bridge

              Am^7
This feeling inside me could never deny me
     D^7 G
The right to be wrong if I choose,
          Gm^7 D
And this pleasure I get from, say, winning a bet
    E^7 C^7 D
Is to lose.

Verse 3

              Bm   F♯^{7}
When I'm drinking my Bonaparte Shandy,
      Bm/A   G^6
Eating more than enough apple pies,
     A^7 D
Will I glance at my screen and see real human beings
        Em$^{(9)}$ Cmaj^7 D
Starve to death right in front of my eyes?

Chorus

             Bm   F♯^{7}
Nothing old, nothing new, nothing ventured,
     Bm/A   G^6
Nothing gained, nothing still-born or lost.
        A^7 D
Nothing further than proof, nothing wilder than youth.
        Em   A^7
Nothing older than time, nothing sweeter than wine,
      F♯^{7} Bm   Bm^7
Nothing physically, recklessly, hopelessly blind,
     G^6 A^7
Nothing I couldn't say, nothing why 'cause today
        D
Nothing rhymed.

Instrumental

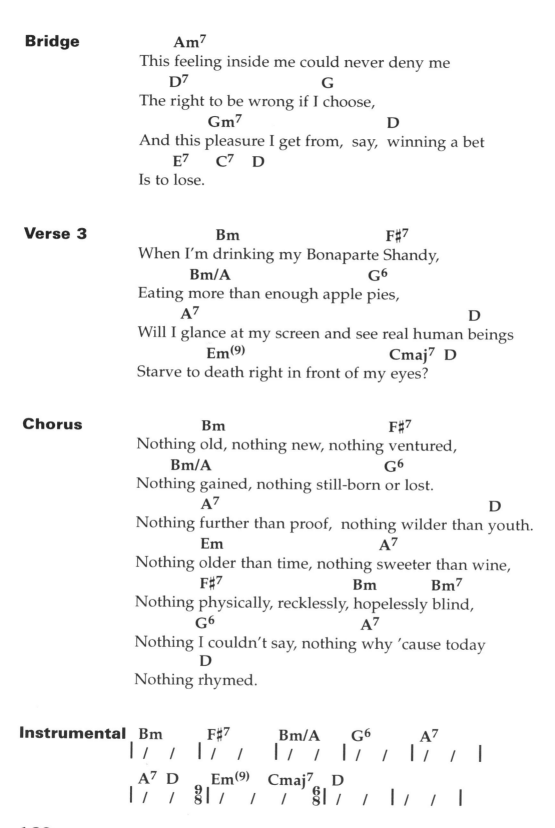

Bridge 2

        Am^7
This feeling inside me could never deny me
    D^7 G
The right to be wrong if I choose,
       Gm^7 D
And this pleasure I get from, say, winning a bet
    E^7 C^7 D
Is to lose.

Chorus 2

       Bm   F♯^{7}
Nothing good, nothing bad, nothing ventured,
    Bm/A   G^6
Nothing gained, nothing still-born or lost.
     A^7 D
Nothing further than proof, nothing wilder than youth.
     Em   A^7
Nothing older than time, nothing sweeter than wine,
     F♯^{7} Bm   Bm^7
Nothing physically, recklessly, hopelessly blind,
    G^6 A^7
Nothing I couldn't say, nothing why 'cause today
    D
Nothing rhymed.

Coda

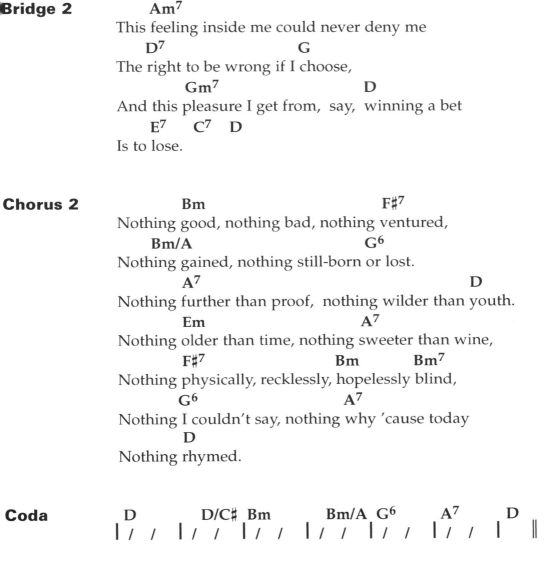

| D | | | D/C♯ | Bm | | Bm/A | G^6 | | A^7 | | D | ‖ |

Proud Mary

Words and Music by
JOHN FOGERTY

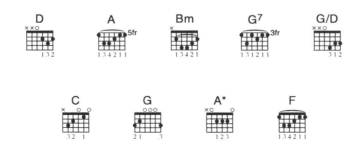

♩ = 94

Intro D
Rolling, rolling, rolling on a river.

(*spoken:* listen to the story now.)

Verse 1 D
Left a good job in the city,

Working for the man every night and day,

And I never lost one minute of sleeping

When I was worrying 'bout the way things might have been.
A
Big wheels keep on turning,
      Bm   G⁷
Ooh the Proud Mary keeps on burning.

Chorus   D
And we're rolling, rolling, rolling on the river.

Rolling on the river.

Verse 2

D
Cleaned a lot of plates in Memphis,

Pumped a lot of tanks down in New Orleans,

But I never saw the good side of the city

Until I hitched a ride on a river boat queen.
A
Big wheels keep on turning.
       Bm   G⁷
Ooh the Proud Mary keeps on burning.

Chorus 2
                        D
And we're rolling, rolling, rolling on the river.

Rolling on the river.

(slower)

Chorus 3   D
Say we're rolling, rolling, rolling on the river.
                  G/D D
Rolling on the ri - ver.

(faster)   ♩ = 166

Link 1   D

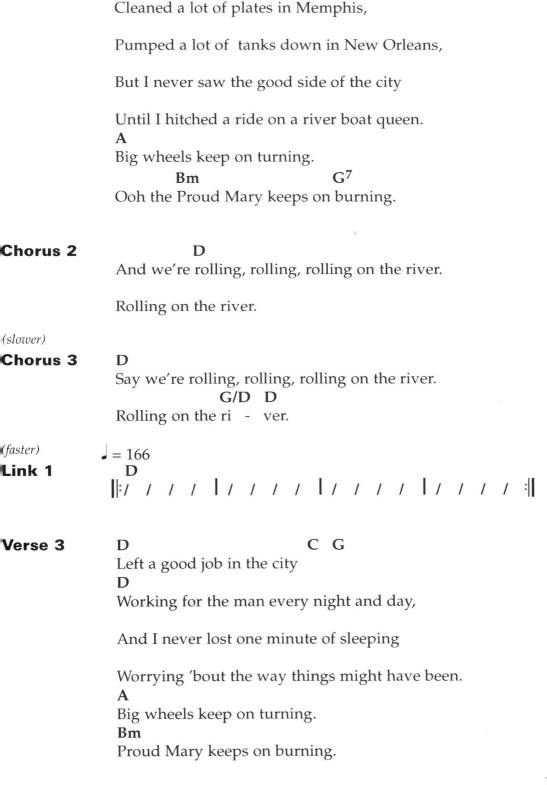

Verse 3   D   C G
Left a good job in the city
D
Working for the man every night and day,

And I never lost one minute of sleeping

Worrying 'bout the way things might have been.
A
Big wheels keep on turning.
Bm
Proud Mary keeps on burning.

Chorus 4   D
Rolling, rolling, rolling on the river.

Rolling, said we're rolling, rolling on the river.

Link 2   D
Move up, toot-toot-toot-toot-toot-toot-toot-toot-

Toot-toot-toot-toot.

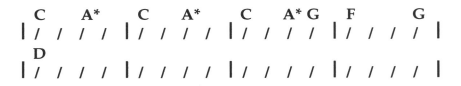

Verse 4   D   C G
Cleaned a lot of plates in Memphis, y'all
D
Pumped a lot of tanks down in New Orleans,

But I never saw the good side of the city

'Til I hitched a ride on a river boat queen.
A
Big wheels keep on turning.
Bm
Proud Mary keeps on burning.

Chorus 5   D
And we're rolling, rolling, rolling on the river.

Said we're rolling, rolling, rolling on the river.

Link 3   D
Move up, toot-toot-toot-toot-toot-toot-toot-toot-

Toot-toot-toot-toot.

```
     C    A*    C    A*     C    A* G   F         G
| /  /  /  /  | /  /  /  /  | /  /  /  /  | /  /  /  /  |
     D
| /  /  /  /  | /  /  /  /  | /  /  /  /  | /  /  /  /  |
```

Verse 5

D   C G
If you come down to the river
   D
I betcha gonna find some people who live.

You don't have to worry if you got no money –

The people on the river are happy to give.
A
Big wheels keep on turning.
Bm
Proud Mary keeps on burning.

Chorus 6

D
‖: Rolling, said we're rolling, rolling on the river. :‖

Link 4

        D
Move up, toot-toot-toot-toot-toot-toot-toot-toot-

Toot-toot-toot-toot.

```
     C    A*    C    A*     C    A* G   F         G
| /  /  /  /  | /  /  /  /  | /  /  /  /  | /  /  /  /  |
     D
| /  /  /  /  | /  /  /  /  | /  /  /  /  | /  /  /  /  |
```

Chorus 7

        D
‖: Rolling, rolling, rolling on the river. :‖ *repeat ad lib. to fade*

Rhinestone Cowboy

Words and Music by
LARRY WEISS

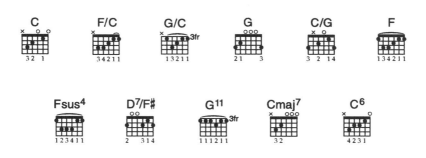

♩ = 112

Intro

```
      C        F/C   G/C   F/C
4 ||: /  /  /   /  | /  /  /   /  :||
4
```

Verse 1

```
            C                      F/C  C     F/C
I've been walking these streets so    long,
C                  F/C         C   F/C
Singing  the same old   song,
   C
I know every crack
   F/C   C       F/C     G           C/G  G  C/G
In these dirty sidewalks of Broadway
       F                      Fsus⁴  F       Fsus⁴
Where hustle's the name of   the      game,
    F                   Fsus⁴  F
And nice guys get washed a - - way
                        C     F/C   C
Like the snow and the rain.
```

Prechorus

        F/C   G   C/G G
There's been a load of compromising
C/G   F   C
On the road to my horizon,
    F D^7/F♯ G^{11} G
But I'm gonna be where the lights are shining on me.

Chorus

N.C. F   G   C   F   C
Like a rhinestone cowboy
      $Cmaj^7$ C^6 G^{11} G
Riding out   on a horse in a star-spangled rodeo.
      F   G   C   F   C
Like a rhinestone cowboy,
      $Cmaj^7$ C^6 G^{11}
Getting cards and letters from people I don't even know.
                      F   C F C F C
And offers coming over the 'phone.

Link

  G   F   G   F   G
| / /   / / | / / / / |

Verse 2

         C   F/C C
Well, I really don't mind the   rain,
F/C   C   F/C   C
And a smile can hide all the pain,
F/C   C   F/C   C
But you're down when you're riding the train
                F   G   C/G   G
That's taking the long   way.
C/G   F $Fsus^4$ F
And I dream of the things I'll   do
$Fsus^4$ F $Fsus^4$ F
With a subway token and   a dollar
                      C   F/C C
Tucked inside my   shoe.

Prechorus 2

                                      G   C/G G   C

There'll be a load of compromising

         F   C

On the road to my horizon,

     F D^7/F♯ G^{11} G

But I'm gonna be where the lights are shining on me.

Chorus 2

N.C. F   G   C   F/C C

Like a rhinestone cowboy

      $Cmaj^7$ C^6 G^{11} G

Riding out   on a horse in a star-spangled rodeo.

F   G   C   F/C C

Rhinestone cowboy,

     $Cmaj^7$ C^6 G^{11}

Getting cards and letters from people I don't even know.

                           F   C F C F C

And offers coming over the   'phone.

Link 2

     G   F   G

| / / / / |

Chorus 3

F   G C   F/C C

Like a rhinestone cowboy

      $Cmaj^7$ C^6 G^{11} G

Riding out   on a horse in a star-spangled rodeo.

      F   G   C   F/C C

Like a rhinestone cowboy,

     $Cmaj^7$ C^6 G^{11}

Getting cards and letters from people I don't even know. *(fade)* ‖

Solid Air

Words and Music by
JOHN MARTYN

Bm⁷   Em⁷   Em⁹   F♯m⁹

Arranged for standard tuning
Capo 1st fret

♩ = 75

Intro

$\frac{4}{4}$ | Bm⁷ / / / / | Em⁷ / / / / | Bm⁷ / / / / | Em⁷ / / / / |

Verse 1

Bm⁷   Em⁷
You've been taking your time
               Bm⁷
And you've been living on   solid air.
               Em⁷
You've been walking the line,
             Bm⁷
And you've been living on solid air.

Prechorus

   Em⁹
Don't know what's going wrong inside,
     F♯m⁹
And I can tell you that it's hard to hide
               Bm⁷
When you're living on_____
   Em⁷   Bm⁷
Solid_____ air._____

Verse 2   Bm^7 Em^7
                You've been painting it blue,
                                                        Bm^7
            You've been looking through   solid air.
                                    Em^7
            You've been seeing it through
                                                    Bm^7
            And you've been looking through   solid air.

Prechorus 2   Em^9
            Don't know what's going wrong in your mind,
                        F♯m^9
            And I can tell you don't like what you find,
                                                Bm^7
            When you're moving through
                    Em^7 Bm^7
            Solid air,_____ solid air.

Bridge   F♯m^9
                I know you, I love you; and I can be your friend,
                                    Em^9
            I could follow you − anywhere.
                    Bm^7 Em^7 Bm^7
            Even through solid air._____

Verse 3   Bm^7 Em^7
                You've been stoning it cold,
                                        Bm^7
            You've been living on   solid air;
                                        Em^7
            You've been finding it cold,
                                    Bm^7
            You've been living on   solid air.

Prechorus 3   Em^9
Don't know what's going wrong inside,
　　　　　　F♯m^9
And I can tell you that it's hard to hide
　　　　　　　　　　　　Bm^7
When you're living on_____
　　　　Em^7　　Bm^7
Solid_____ air._____

Verse 4   Bm^7　　　　　　　　　　　　Em^7
　　　You've been getting too deep,
　　　　　　　　Bm^7
You've been living on　　solid air.
　　　　　　　　　　　Em^7
You've been missing your sleep
　　　　　　　　　　　　　　Bm^7
And you've been moving through solid air.

Prechorus 4   Em^9
Don't know what's going wrong in your mind,
　　　F♯m^9
But I know you don't like what you find,
　　　　　　　　　　　　　　Bm^7
When you're moving through
　　　Em^7　Bm^7
Solid air,_____ solid air.

Bridge 2   F♯m^9
　　　I know you, I love you; I'll be your friend,
　　　　　　　Em^9
I could follow you – anywhere.
　　　　　　Bm^7　　　Em^7　Bm^7
Even through　　solid air.

Verse 5

Bm^7 Em^7
You've been walking your line,
Bm^7
You've been walking on solid air;
Em^7
You've been taking your time
Bm^7
'Cause you've been walking on solid air.

Prechorus 5

Em^9
Don't know what's going wrong inside,
F♯m^9
But I can tell you that it's hard to hide,
Bm^7
When you're living on
Em^7 Bm^7
Solid air,_____ solid air.

Verse 6

Bm^7 Em^7
You've been painting it blue,
Bm^7
You've been living on solid air.
Em^7
You've been seeing it through
Bm^7
And you've been living on solid air.

Prechorus 6

Em^9
Don't know what's going wrong in your mind,
F♯m^9
And I can tell you don't like what you find,
Bm^7
When you're living on
Em^7 Bm^7
Solid air,_____ solid air.

Bridge 3 F#m^9

I know you, I love you; and I'll be your friend,

Em^9

I could follow you – anywhere.

Bm^7 Em^7 Bm^7

Even through   solid air.

Em^7 Bm^7 Em^7

I see ooh,   solid air._____

Coda
(vocal ad lib.)

Bm^7 Em^7 x5

‖: / / / / | / / / / :‖

Bm^7

| / / / / | / / / / | / / / / | / / / / ‖

Son Of My Father

Words by PETER BELLOTTE AND MICHAEL HOLM
Music by GIORGIO MORODER

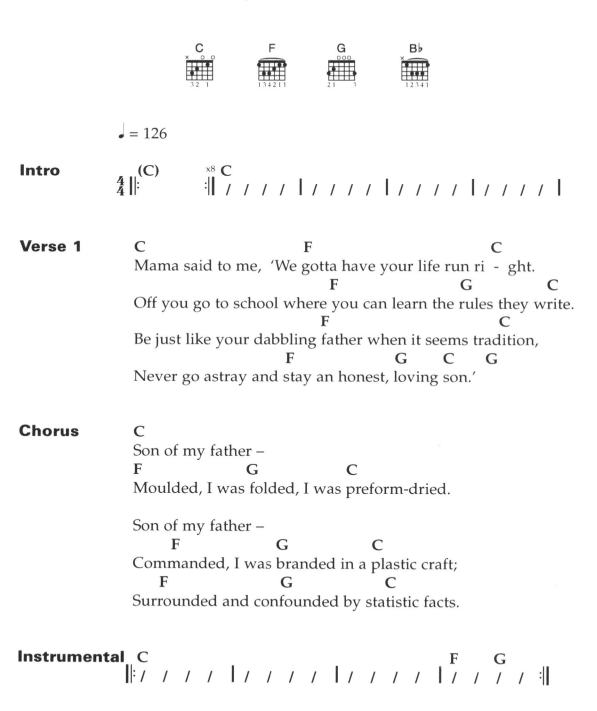

♩ = 126

Intro

Verse 1

    C   **F**   **C**
Mama said to me, 'We gotta have your life run ri - ght.
                                 F   **G**   **C**
Off you go to school where you can learn the rules they write.
                         F   **C**
Be just like your dabbling father when it seems tradition,
                  F   **G**   **C** **G**
Never go astray and stay an honest, loving son.'

Chorus

    C
Son of my father –
F   **G**   **C**
Moulded, I was folded, I was preform-dried.

Son of my father –
     F   **G**   **C**
Commanded, I was branded in a plastic craft;
    F   **G**   **C**
Surrounded and confounded by statistic facts.

Instrumental **C**   **F**   **G**

```
  C              F                        Bb   C
| / / / / | / / / / | / / / / | / / / / |

  F              C                        F    G
| / / / / | / / / / | / / / / | / / / / |
```

Link

```
 (C)
||: / / / / | / / / / | / / / / | / / / / :||
```

Verse 2

```
C                        F                    C
Tried to let me in but I jumped out of my skin in time.
                  F         G C
I scrutinized and read the alibi  signs.
                        F              C
So I left my home, I'm really on my own at last:
                        F       G       C       G
Left the trodden path and separated from the past.
```

Chorus 2

```
C
Son of my father –
F           G           C
Changing, rearranging into someone new.

Son of my father –
    F           G           C
Collecting and selecting independent views,
F               G           C           G
Knowing and I'm showing how a change is due.
```

Chorus 3

```
C
Son of my father –
F           G           C
Moulded, I was folded, I was preform-dried.

Son of my father –
    F               G           C
Commanded, I was branded in a plastic craft,
    F               G           C
Surrounded and confounded by statistic facts.   (fade)
```

Song To The Siren

Words and Music by
TIM BUCKLEY AND LARRY BECKETT

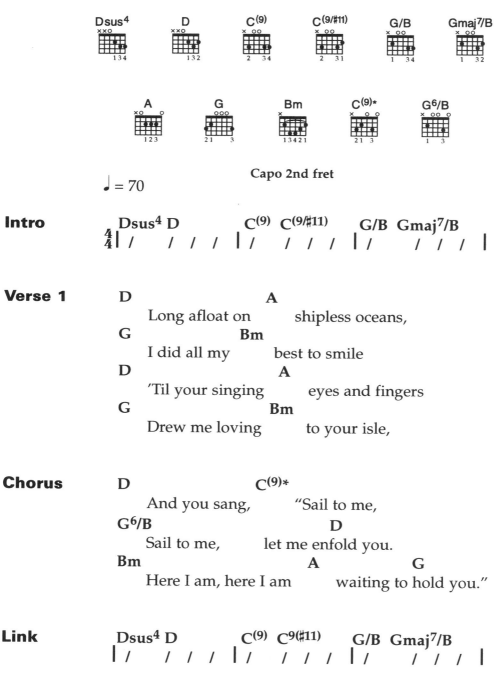

Capo 2nd fret

$\natural = 70$

Intro

$\frac{4}{4}$ | Dsus⁴ D / / / / | C⁽⁹⁾ C⁽⁹/♯11⁾ / / / | G/B Gmaj⁷/B / / / |

Verse 1

D   A
Long afloat on   shipless oceans,
G   Bm
I did all my   best to smile
D   A
'Til your singing   eyes and fingers
G   Bm
Drew me loving   to your isle,

Chorus

D   C⁽⁹⁾*
And you sang,   "Sail to me,
G⁶/B   D
Sail to me,   let me enfold you.
Bm   A   G
Here I am, here I am   waiting to hold you."

Link

| Dsus⁴ D / / / / | C⁽⁹⁾ C9⁽♯11⁾ / / / | G/B Gmaj⁷/B / / / |

Verse 2

D   A
Did I dream you   dreamed about me?
G   Bm
Were you hare when   I was fox?
D   A
Now my foolish   boat is leaning
G   Bm
Broken, lovelorn   on your rocks,

Chorus 2

D $C^{(9)}$*
For you sing,   "Touch me not,
G^6/B
Touch me not,   come back tomorrow: D
Bm   A   G
Oh my heart, oh my heart   shies from the sorrow."

Link

Dsus^4 D $C^{(9)}$ $C9^{(\sharp 11)}$ G/B Gmaj^7/B
| /   / / / | /   / / / | /   / / / |

Verse 3

D   A
I am puzzled   as the oyster,
G   Bm
I am troubled   as the tide:
D   A
Should I stand   amid your breakers,
G   Bm
Or should I lie   with   death my bride?

Chorus 3

D $C^{(9)}$*
Hear me sing,   "Swim to me,
G^6/B   D
Swim to me,   let me enfold you:
Bm   A   G
Here I am, here I am,   waiting to hold you."

Spirit In The Sky

Words and Music by
NORMAN GREENBAUM

♩ = 126

Intro

$\begin{array}{l}\text{A*} \qquad\qquad\qquad \text{D}^5 \text{ C}^5 \text{ A*} \qquad\qquad\qquad \text{C}^5 \text{ D}^5 \text{ x4}\end{array}$

$\frac{4}{4}$ ‖: / / / / | / / / / | / / / / | / / / / :‖

Verse 1

A
 When I die and they lay me to rest
             D
 Gonna go to the place that's best,
                 A
 When they lay me down to die
         E   A
 Going up to the spirit in the sky.

Chorus

A
 Going up to the spirit in the sky (spirit in the sky) –
                 D
 That's where I'm gonna go when I die (when I die).
                 A
 When I die and they lay me to rest
         E   A
 I'm gonna go to the place that's the best.

Link

$\begin{array}{l}\text{A*} \qquad\qquad\qquad \text{D}^5 \text{ C}^5 \text{ A*} \qquad\qquad\qquad \text{C}^5 \text{ D}^5\end{array}$

‖: / / / / | / / / / | / / / / | / / / / :‖

Verse 2

    A
Prepare yourself, you know it's a must –
         D
Gotta have a friend in Jesus.
        A
So you know that when you die
  E   A
He's gonna recommend you to the spirit in the sky

(Spirit in the sky).

Chorus 2

    A
Oh, recommend you to the spirit in the sky,
               D
That's where you're gonna go when you die – (when you die).
        A
When you die and they lay you to rest
    E   A
You're gonna go to the place that's the best.

Link 2

A^* D^5 C^5 A^* C^5 D^5
‖: / / / / | / / / / | / / / / | / / / / :‖

Guitar solo

A   G   A   C
| / / / / | / / / / | / / / / | / / / / |
A   G   A   C   D
| / / / / | / / / / | / / / / | / / / / |

Link 3

A^* D^5 C^5 A^* C^5 D^5
‖: / / / / | / / / / | / / / / | / / / / :‖

Verse 3

A
Never been a sinner, I've never sinned;
                D
I've got a friend in Jesus.
            A
So you know that when I die
    E   A
He's gonna set me up with the spirit in the sky.

Chorus 3

A
Oh, set me up with the spirit in the sky – (spirit in the sky)
                      D
That's where I'm gonna go when I die – (when I die).
            A
When I die and they lay me to rest
      E   A
I'm gonna go to the place that's the best,
E   A
Go to the place that's the best.

Coda

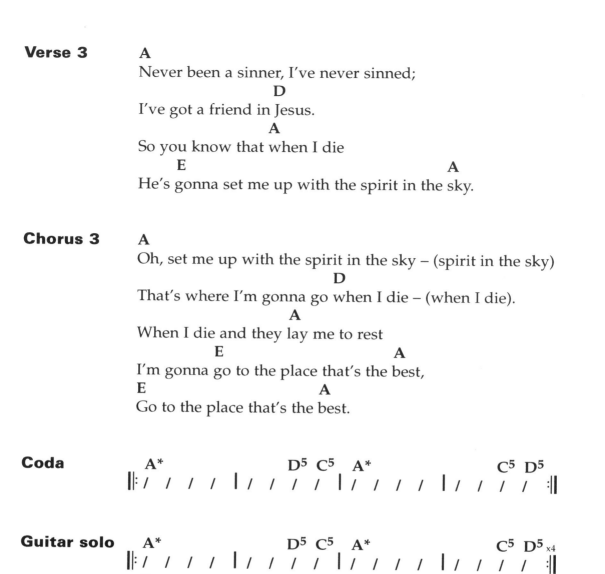

Guitar solo

180

Stairway To Heaven

Words and Music by
JIMMY PAGE AND ROBERT PLANT

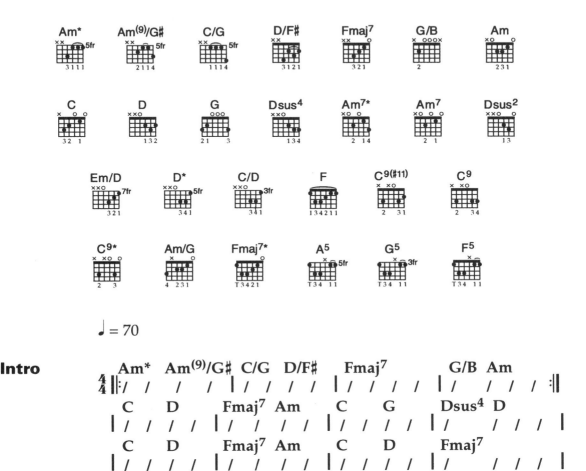

♩ = 70

Intro

Am* Am⁽⁹⁾/G♯ C/G D/F♯   Fmaj⁷   G/B Am

C   D   Fmaj⁷ Am   C   G   Dsus⁴ D

C   D   Fmaj⁷ Am   C   D   Fmaj⁷

Verse 1

        Am*   Am⁽⁹⁾/G♯
There's a lady who's sure
     C/G   D/F♯
All that glitters is gold
      Fmaj⁷   G/B Am
And she's buying a stairway to Hea - ven.

$$\text{Am* \qquad\qquad Am}^{(9)}\text{/G}\sharp$$
When she gets there she knows
$$\text{C/G \qquad\qquad D/F}\sharp$$
If the stores are all closed
$$\text{Fmaj}^7 \qquad\qquad\qquad \text{G/B \quad Am}$$
With a word she can get what she came for.

Bridge 1 C   D   Fmaj⁷ Am
Ooh,_____ ooh_____
                    C   G   Dsus⁴ D
And she's buying a stairway to Hea - ven.
                    C   D
There's a sign on the wall
            Fmaj⁷   Am
But she wants to be sure
                    C   D   Fmaj⁷
'Cause you know sometimes words have two meanings.

Verse 2   Am*   Am⁽⁹⁾/G♯
In a tree by the brook
                    C/G   D/F♯
There's a songbird who sings,
                    Fmaj⁷   G/B Am
Sometimes all of our thoughts are misgiv - - en.

Link 1   Am*   Am⁽⁹⁾/G♯ C/G D/F♯   Fmaj⁷   G/B Am   G
| / /   /   /   / | / /   /   / | / /   /   / | /   / / / |

Link 2   Am⁷*   Am⁷ Dsus²   D   Am⁷*   Am⁷
| / / / / / | Ooh,_____ it makes me wonder.
    Em/D D* C/D D*
| /   /   / / |

    Am⁷* Am⁷ Dsus² D   Am⁷* Am⁷
Ooh,_____   it makes me wonder._____
    Em/D D* C/D D*
| /   /   / / |

182

Verse 3

                            C   G/B   Am
There's a feeling I get when I look to the west
                        C   G/B   F Am
And my spirit is crying for leaving.
                    C   G/B   Am
In my thoughts I have seen rings of smoke through the trees
                          C   G/B   F Am   C G/B
And the voices of those who stand looking. | / / / / |

Link 3

   Am^{7}*   Am^{7} Dsus^{2} D
| / / / / / | Ooh,_____ it makes me wonder.
   Am^{7}*   Am^{7} Em/D D* C/D D*
| / / / / / | /   /   /   / |

   Am^{7}* Am^{7} Dsus^{2} D
Ooh,_____ it really makes me wonder.
   Am^{7}*   Am^{7} Em/D D* C/D D*
| / / / / | /   /   /   / |

Verse 4

                        C   G/B   Am
And it's whispered that soon if we all call the tune
                        C   G/B   F Am
Then the piper will lead us to reason,
                     C   G/B   Am
And a new day will dawn for those who stand long
                         C   G/B   F   Am   C   G/B
And the forests will echo with laughter. | / / / / |

Link 4

   Am^{7}*   Am^{7} Dsus^{2} D   Am^{7}*   Am^{7} Em/D D* C/D D*
| / / / / | / / / / | / / / / | /   /   /   / |
   Am^{7}*   Am^{7} Dsus^{2} D
| / / / / | Oh,_____ oh.
   Am^{7}*   Am^{7} Em/D D* C/D D*
| / / / / | /   /   /   / |

Verse 5

C   G/B   Am
If there's a bustle in your hedgerow don't be alarmed now
C   G/B   F   Am
It's just a spring-clean for the May Queen.
C   G/B   Am
Yes there are two paths you can go by but in the long run
C   G/B   F   Am   C   G/B
There's still time to change the road you're on. | / / / / |

Link 5

Am^{7}*   Am^{7} Dsus^{2} D   Am^{7}*   Am^{7}
| / / / / | And it makes me wonder.
Em/D D* C/D D*
| /   /   /   / |
Am^{7}*   Am^{7} Dsus^{2} D
| / / / / | Ah._____
Am^{7}*   Am^{7} Em/D D* C/D D*
| / / / / | /   /   /   / |

Verse 6

C   G/B   Am
Your head is humming and it won't go –

In case you don't know –
C   G/B   F   Am
The piper's calling you to join him.
C   G/B   Am
Dear lady, can you hear the wind blow? And did you know
C   G/B   F   Am   C   G/B
Your stairway lies on the whispering wind. | / / / / |
D   Dsus^{2} D Dsus^{4} Dsus^{2} D Dsus^{4} Dsus^{2} D Dsus^{4} D
| / / / / | /   /   /   / $\frac{3}{4}$| / / / |

'Fanfare'

C C9(#11) C9 C C9(#11) C9 Dsus2 D
4/4 | / / / / | 5/4 / / / / / |

Dsus4 Dsus2 D Dsus4 Dsus2 D Dsus4 D
4/4 | / / / / / | 3/4 / / / |

C C9(#11) C9* G/B
4/4 | / / / / / | / / / / / ‖

Guitar solo Am Am/G Fmaj7* Am Am/G Fmaj7* x5
‖: / / / / / | / / / / / | / / / / / | / / / / / :‖

Verse 7

A5   G5   F5   G5
And as we wind on down the road,

A5   G5   F5   G5
Our shadows taller than our souls,

A5   G5   F5   G5
There walks a lady we all know

A5   G5   F5   G5
Who shines white light and wants to show

A5   G5   F5   G5
How everything still turns to gold,

A5   G5   F5   G5
And if you listen very hard

A5   G5   F5   G5
The tune will come to you at last:

A5   G5   Fmaj7*
When all are one and one is   all,

A5   G5   Fmaj7*
To be a rock and not to   roll.____

Am Am/G Fmaj7* Am Am/G Fmaj7
| / / / / / | / / / / / | / / / / / | / / / / / |

Coda

Am Am/G Fmaj7 Am Am/G
| / / / / / | / / / / / | / / / / / |

Fmaj7   N.C.
And she's buying a stairway to Heaven. ‖

185

Stand By Your Man

Words and Music by
BILLY SHERRILL AND TAMMY WYNETTE

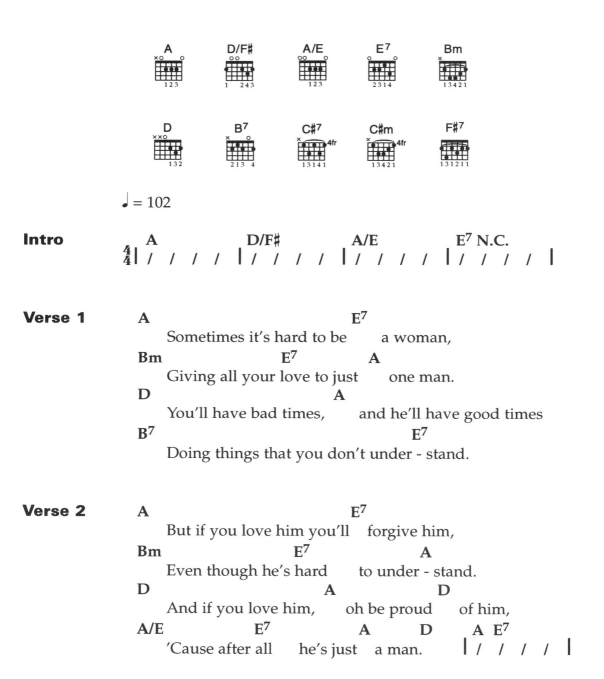

♩ = 102

Intro

$\frac{4}{4}$ | A / / / / | D/F♯ / / / / | A/E / / / / | E⁷ N.C. / / / / |

Verse 1

A   E⁷
Sometimes it's hard to be a woman,
Bm   E⁷   A
Giving all your love to just one man.
D   A
You'll have bad times, and he'll have good times
B⁷   E⁷
Doing things that you don't under - stand.

Verse 2

A   E⁷
But if you love him you'll forgive him,
Bm   E⁷   A
Even though he's hard to under - stand.
D   A   D
And if you love him, oh be proud of him,
A/E   E⁷   A D A E⁷
'Cause after all he's just a man. | / / / / |

Chorus

A   C#7
Stand by your man,
D   C#m Bm
Give him two arms to cling to,
A   F#7
And something warm to come to
B7   E7   N.C.
When nights are cold and lonely.
A   C#7
Stand by your man,
D   C#m Bm
And show the world you love him.
A   E7   C#7   F#7
Keep giving all the love you can.
D   E7   A   D   A E7
Stand by your man. | / / / / |

Chorus 2

A   C#7
Stand by your man,
D   C#m Bm
And show the world you love him.
A   E7   C#7   F#7
Keep giving all the love you can _____
D   E7   A   D/F#   A/E   Bm E7   A
Stand by your man._____ | ||

Starman

**Words and Music by
DAVID BOWIE**

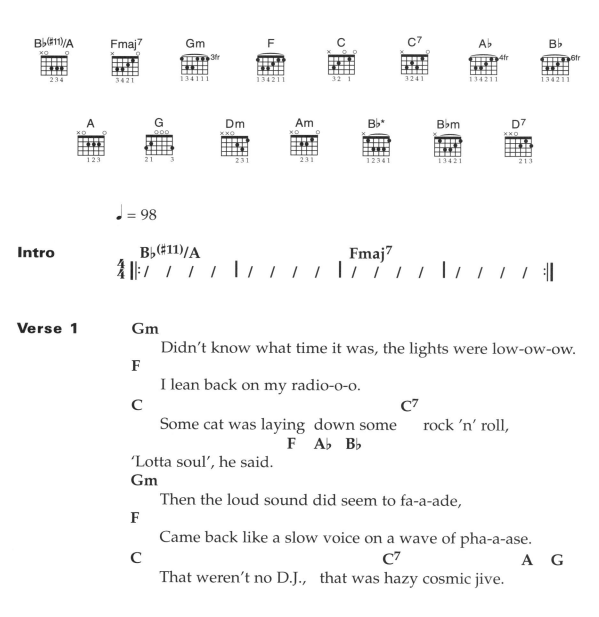

♩ = 98

Intro

Bb(#11)/A   Fmaj7

Verse 1

Gm
    Didn't know what time it was, the lights were low-ow-ow.
F
    I lean back on my radio-o-o.
C   C7
    Some cat was laying down some   rock 'n' roll,
                      F Ab Bb
'Lotta soul', he said.
Gm
    Then the loud sound did seem to fa-a-ade,
F
    Came back like a slow voice on a wave of pha-a-ase.
C   C7   A G
    That weren't no D.J.,   that was hazy cosmic jive.

Chorus

             F   Dm
There's a starman waiting in the sky –
      Am   C
He'd like to come and meet us
       C^7
But he thinks he'd blow our minds.
         F   Dm
There's a starman waiting in the sky –
     Am   C
He's told us not to blow it
                   C^7
'Cause he knows it's all worthwhile,
        Bb*   Bbm   F D^7
He told me: "Let the children lose it,   let the children use it,
Gm   C
    Let all the children boogie."

Link 1

    Bb*   F   C   F
| / / / / | / / / / | / / / / | / / / / |
    Bb*   F   C
| / / / / | / / / / | / / / / ‖

Verse 2

Gm
    Well I had to phone someone so I picked on you-ou-ou,
F
    Hey, that's far out! So you heard him too-oo-oo!
C
    Switch on the T.V.,
        C^7 F Ab Bb
We may pick him up on channel 2.
Gm
    Look out your window I can see his li-i-ight,
F
    If we can sparkle he may land toni-i-ight.
C C^7 A G
    Don't tell your papa or he'll get us locked up in fright.

Chorus 2

            F   Dm
There's a starman waiting in the sky –
      Am   C
He'd like to come and meet us
         C⁷
But he thinks he'd blow our minds.
           F   Dm
There's a starman waiting in the sky –
      Am   C
He's told us not to blow it
                       C⁷
'Cause he knows it's all worthwhile,
         Bb*   Bbm   F   D⁷
He told me: "Let the children lose it,   let the children use it,
Gm   C
    Let all the children boogie."

Chorus 3

      F   Dm
Starman waiting in the sky –
      Am   C
He'd like to come and meet us
         C⁷
But he thinks he'd blow our minds
        F   Dm
There's a starman waiting in the sky –
      Am   C
He's told us not to blow it
                C⁷
'Cause he knows it's all worthwhile,
         Bb*   Bbm   F   D⁷
He told me: "Let the children lose it,   let the children use it,
Gm   C
    Let all the children boogie."

Coda

     Bb*   F   C   F
| / / / / | / / / / | / / / / | / / / / ‖

     Bb*   F   C   F
‖: La,   la, la, la, la,   la, la, la,   la,   la, la, la, la, la, la, la. :‖

repeat to fade

Take It Easy

Words and Music by
GLENN FREY AND JACKSON BROWNE

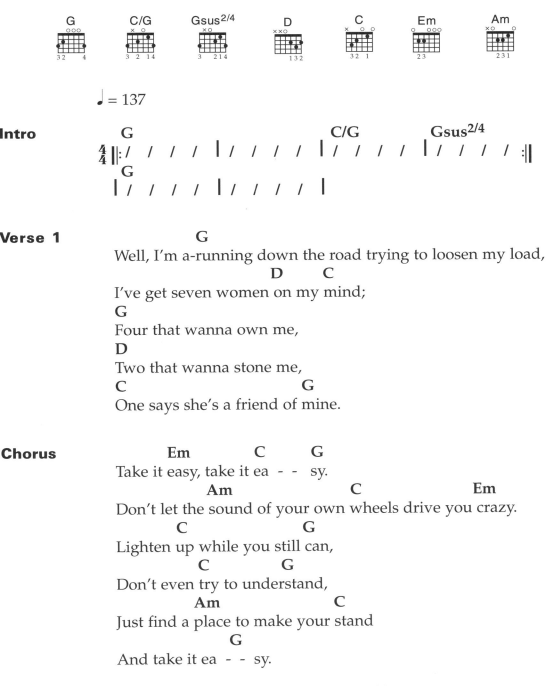

Intro

Verse 1

G
Well, I'm a-running down the road trying to loosen my load,
           D   C
I've get seven women on my mind;
G
Four that wanna own me,
D
Two that wanna stone me,
C   G
One says she's a friend of mine.

Chorus

         Em   C   G
Take it easy, take it ea - - sy.
                 Am   C   Em
Don't let the sound of your own wheels drive you crazy.
         C   G
Lighten up while you still can,
         C   G
Don't even try to understand,
                 Am   C
Just find a place to make your stand
                 G
And take it ea - - sy.

Verse 2

                   G

Well, I'm a-standing on a corner in Winslow, Arizona,

             D   C

And such a fine sight to see.

       G   D

It's a girl, my Lord, in a flatbed Ford

       C   G

Slowing down to take a look at me.

Chorus 2

           Em D   C   G

Come on, ba - - by, don't say may - be.

       Am   C   Em

I gotta know if your sweet love is gonna save me.

     C   G

We may lose and we may win,

               C   G

Though we will never be here again.

       Am   C

So open up, I'm climbing in,

           G

So take it ea - - sy.

Guitar solo

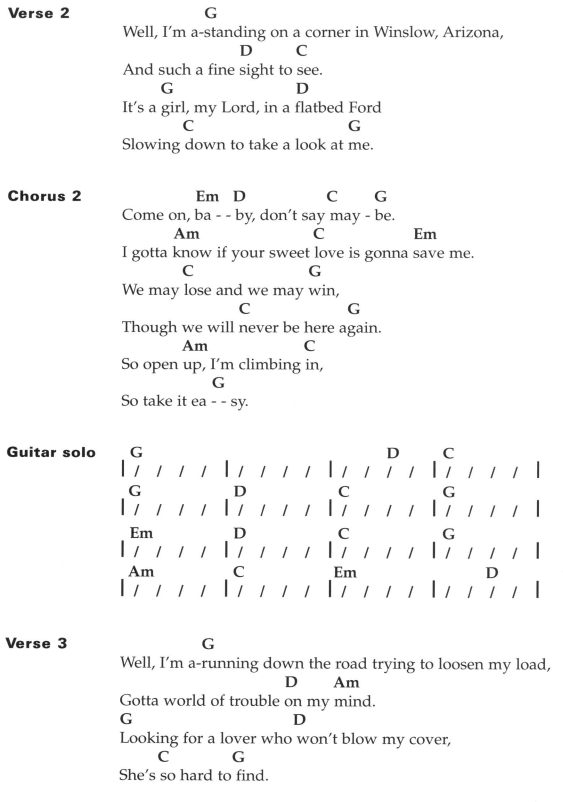

Verse 3

                  G

Well, I'm a-running down the road trying to loosen my load,

                       D   Am

Gotta world of trouble on my mind.

G   D

Looking for a lover who won't blow my cover,

       C   G

She's so hard to find.

Chorus 3
              Em   C   G
Take it easy, take it ea - - sy.
                      Am   C   Em
Don't let the sound of your own wheels make you crazy.
            C   G   C   G
Come on, ba - by, don't say may - be.
          Am   C   G   N.C.
I gotta know if your sweet love is gonna save me.

Coda
          C   G
Ooh, ooh, ooh, ooh.
          C   G
Ooh, ooh, ooh, ooh.
          C   G $Gsus^{2/4}$ C
Ooh, ooh, oh, we got it ea - - - - - sy.
                            G $Gsus^{2/4}$
We ought to take it ea - - - -
  C   Em
| / / / / | / / / / | / ‖
(-sy.)

Tequila Sunrise

Words and Music by
DON HENLEY AND GLENN FREY

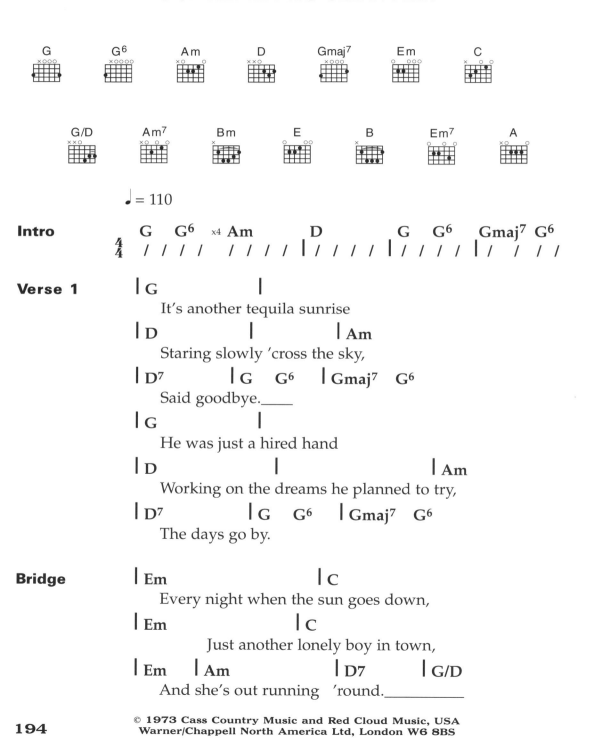

Intro

G G⁶ x4 Am   D   G G⁶ Gmaj⁷ G⁶

$\frac{4}{4}$ / / / / / / / / | / / / / | / / / / | / / / /

Verse 1

| G |
It's another tequila sunrise

| D | | Am
Staring slowly 'cross the sky,

| D⁷ | G G⁶ | Gmaj⁷ G⁶
Said goodbye.____

| G |
He was just a hired hand

| D | | Am
Working on the dreams he planned to try,

| D⁷ | G G⁶ | Gmaj⁷ G⁶
The days go by.

Bridge

| Em | C
Every night when the sun goes down,

| Em | C
Just another lonely boy in town,

| Em | Am | D7 | G/D
And she's out running 'round._____

Verse 2

```
| G                    |
    She wasn't just another woman
| D              |              | Am
    And I couldn't keep  from coming on,
| D7          | G   G6   | Gmaj7  G6
    It's been so long.
| G               |
    Oh and it's a hollow feeling
| D              |              | Am
    When it comes down to dealing friends
| D7        | G   G6   | Gmaj7  G6
    It never ends.
```

Guitar solo

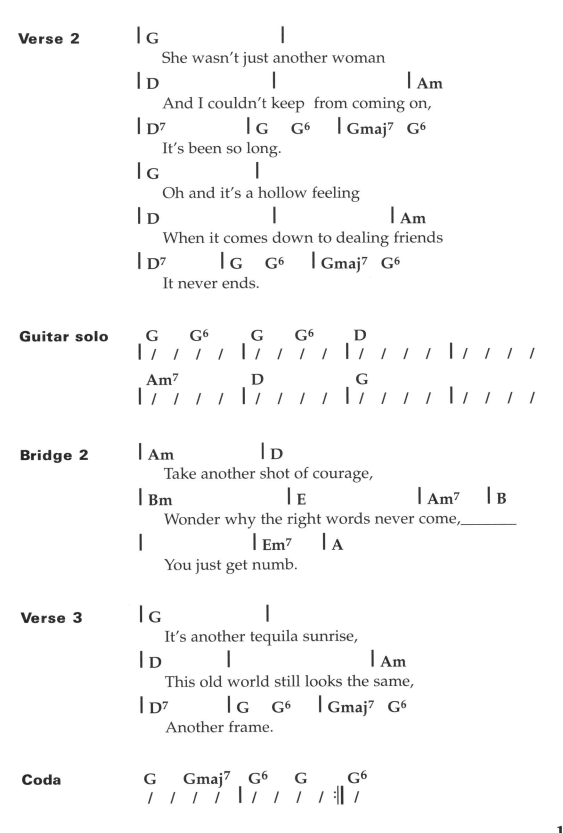

```
  G     G6      G     G6      D
| / / / / / | / / / / / | / / / / / | / / / / /

  Am7           D           G
| / / / / / | / / / / / | / / / / / | / / / / /
```

Bridge 2

```
| Am          | D
    Take another shot of courage,
| Bm              | E              | Am7    | B
    Wonder why the right words never come,_____
|                | Em7    | A
    You just get numb.
```

Verse 3

```
| G               |
    It's another tequila sunrise,
| D        |              | Am
    This old world still looks the same,
| D7        | G   G6   | Gmaj7  G6
    Another frame.
```

Coda

```
  G   Gmaj7  G6   G      G6
  / / / / | / / / / / :|| /
```

Take Me Home, Country Roads

Words and Music by
JOHN DENVER, BILL DANOFF AND TAFFY NIVERT

A   F#m   E   D   G   E^7 D/A

$\downarrow$ = 80

Intro

$\frac{4}{4}$ | A / / / / | / / / / |

Verse 1

```
A                        F#m
  Almost Heaven,           West Virginia,
E                                   D          A
  Blue Ridge Mountains,      Shenandoah river.
                          F#m
Life is old there,      older than the trees,
E
Younger than the mountains,
D            A
Growing like a breeze.
```

Chorus

          A   E
Country roads, take me home
      F♯m   D
To the place I belong:
          A   E
West Virginia, mountain momma,
        D   A
Take me home, country roads.

Verse 2

A   F♯m
   All my memories   gather 'round her
E   D   A
   Miner's lady,   stranger to blue water.
               F♯m
Dark and dusty, painted on the sky,
E
Misty taste of moonshine;
D   A
Teardrop in my eye.

Chorus 2

          A   E
Country roads, take me home
      F♯m   D
To the place I belong:
          A   E
West Virginia, mountain momma,
        D   A
Take me home, country roads.

Bridge

F♯m   E
   I hear her voice,
      A
In the morning hour she calls me.
        D   A   E
The radio reminds me of my home far away,
      F♯m   G   D
And driving down the road I get a feeling
        A E^7
That I should have been home yesterday, yesterday.

Chorus 3

          A   E
Country roads, take me home
       F♯m   D
To the place I belong:
        A   E
West Virginia, mountain momma,
      D   A
Take me home, country roads.

Chorus 4

          A   E
Country roads, take me home
       F♯m   D
To the place I belong:
        A   E
West Virginia, mountain momma,
      D   A
Take me home, country roads.

Coda

         E   A
Take me home, down country roads,
         E   A   D/A A
Take me home, down country roads.   ‖

We Will

Words and Music by
RAYMOND O'SULLIVAN

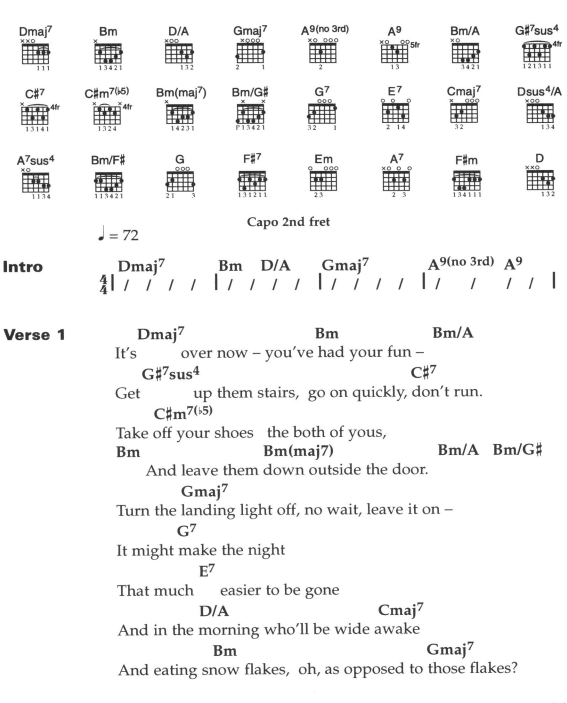

Capo 2nd fret

$\downarrow$ = 72

Intro

Dmaj⁷   Bm   D/A   Gmaj⁷   A⁹(no 3rd)   A⁹

4/4 | / / / / | / / / / | / / / / | / / / / |

Verse 1

        Dmaj⁷   Bm   Bm/A
It's   over now – you've had your fun –
      G♯⁷sus⁴   C♯⁷
Get   up them stairs, go on quickly, don't run.
      C♯m⁷(♭5)
Take off your shoes   the both of yous,
Bm   Bm(maj7)   Bm/A   Bm/G♯
      And leave them down outside the door.
      Gmaj⁷
Turn the landing light off, no wait, leave it on –
      G⁷
It might make the night
        E⁷
That much   easier to be gone
          D/A   Cmaj⁷
And in the morning who'll be wide awake
          Bm   Gmaj⁷
And eating snow flakes, oh, as opposed to those flakes?

Chorus

    D/A   Dsus⁴/A
(We will) we will
   A⁷sus⁴   A⁹
(We will) we will.

Verse 2

    Dmaj⁷   Bm   Bm/A
That   afternoon we spent the day
   G♯⁷sus⁴   C♯⁷
With   uncle Frank (remember?) and his wife aunty May.
   C♯m⁷⁽♭⁵⁾
Well, do you know since then I've received up to four letters
Bm   Bm(maj7) Bm/A Bm/G♯
  All of which repeat the same:_____
    Gmaj⁷
They say, 'thrilled to bits' – 'can't believe you came' –
    G⁷   E⁷
'We've relived it both over time and time again,
     D/A   Cmaj⁷
And if there's ever a chance or even half
       Bm   Gmaj⁷
You might be our___ way, then would you promise to stay?'

Chorus 2

    D/A   Dsus⁴/A
(We will) we will
   A⁷sus⁴   A⁹
(We will) we will.

Bridge

     Bm/F♯ G   C♯⁷ F♯⁷
Oh it's not easy pretending that you cannot hear
      Bm Em A⁷   D
Once you've suffered the affliction within.
    F♯m   G   D/A   Bm
It's no use in an ending to proclaim from the start
    Bm/G♯   A⁹⁽ⁿᵒ ³ʳᵈ⁾ A⁹
That the moral of the story's to begin.

Verse 3

Dmaj^7 Bm   Bm/A
On   Sunday next if the weather holds
   G♯^{7}sus^4 C♯^{7}
We'll   have that game – but I bagsy being in goal.
     C♯m$^{7(♭5)}$
Not because I'm good, or because I think I should,
    Bm   Bm(maj7)   Bm/A   Bm/G♯
It's just that –   well, at my age I think standing still
        Gmaj^7
Would really   suit me best – do we all agree?
     G^7 E^7
Hands up those who do, hands up   those who don't.
       D/A   Cmaj^7
I see. Well, in that case, will we please be kind enough
    Bm   Gmaj^7
If not on Sunday,   to go to Mass on Monday?

Chorus 3

D/A   Dsus^4/A
(We will) we will
   A^{7}sus^4 A^9
(We will) we will, yeah,   yeah, yeah,
   D
We will. ‖

Wish You Were Here

Words and Music by
GEORGE ROGER WATERS AND DAVID GILMOUR

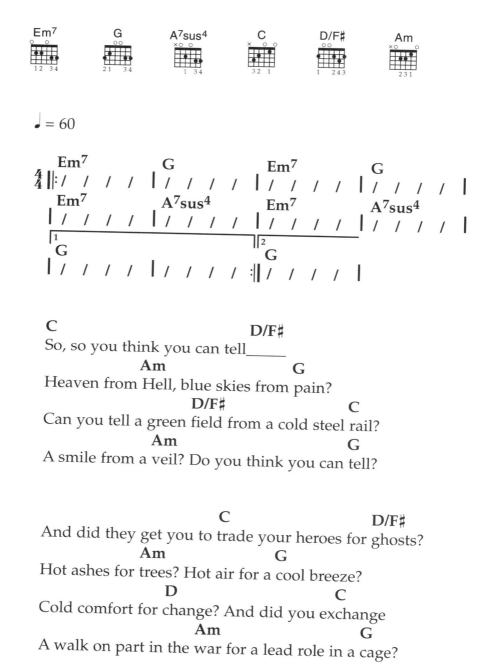

Intro

Verse 1

C   D/F♯
So, so you think you can tell_____
                 Am   G
Heaven from Hell, blue skies from pain?
                    D/F♯   C
Can you tell a green field from a cold steel rail?
                Am   G
A smile from a veil? Do you think you can tell?

Verse 2

                         C   D/F♯
And did they get you to trade your heroes for ghosts?
            Am   G
Hot ashes for trees? Hot air for a cool breeze?
            D   C
Cold comfort for change? And did you exchange
                 Am   G
A walk on part in the war for a lead role in a cage?

Guitar solo

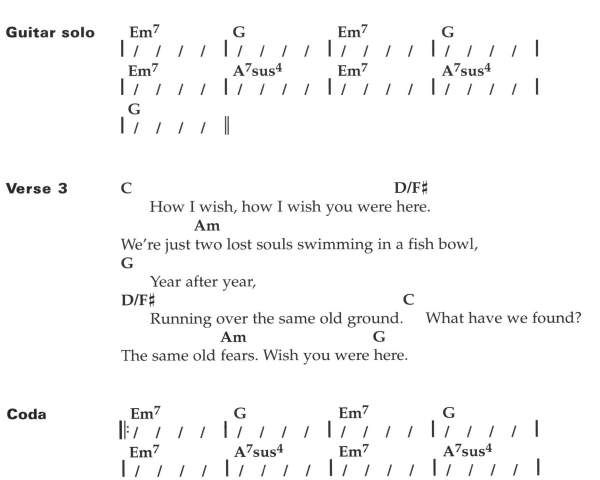

```
 Em7         G           Em7         G
| / / / /   | / / / /   | / / / /   | / / / / |
 Em7         A7sus4      Em7         A7sus4
| / / / /   | / / / /   | / / / /   | / / / / |
 G
| / / / /   ||
```

Verse 3

```
C                                          D/F#
     How I wish, how I wish you were here.
             Am
We're just two lost souls swimming in a fish bowl,
G
     Year after year,
D/F#                                           C
     Running over the same old ground.    What have we found?
               Am                        G
The same old fears. Wish you were here.
```

Coda

```
 Em7         G           Em7         G
||: / / / / | / / / /   | / / / /   | / / / / |
 Em7         A7sus4      Em7         A7sus4
| / / / /   | / / / /   | / / / /   | / / / / |
 G
| / / / /   | / / / /  :||  repeat to fade
```

Year Of The Cat

Words and Music by
PETER WOOD AND AL STEWART

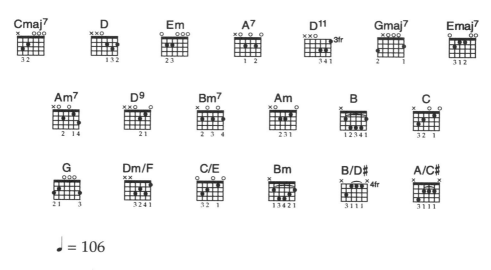

♩ = 106

Intro

Cmaj⁷ D   Em   D   Cmaj⁷ D   Em   D

Cmaj⁷ D   Em   A⁷   D¹¹

Gmaj⁷   Cmaj⁷   Gmaj⁷   Cmaj⁷

Emaj⁷   Am⁷   D⁹

Cmaj⁷ D   Em   D   Cmaj⁷ D   Em   D

Cmaj⁷ D   Em   A⁷   D¹¹

Verse 1

Cmaj^7 Bm^7 Em
On a morning from a Bogart movie
Cmaj^7 Bm^7 Em
In a country where they turn back time,
Cmaj^7 Bm^7 Em
You go strolling through the crowd like Peter Lorre
Am D
Contemplating a crime.
Cmaj^7 Bm^7 Em
She comes out of the sun in a silk dress running
B C
Like a water-colour in the rain.
B Em
Don't bother asking for explanations –
Am^7
She'll just tell you that she came
D^9
In the year of the cat.

Link

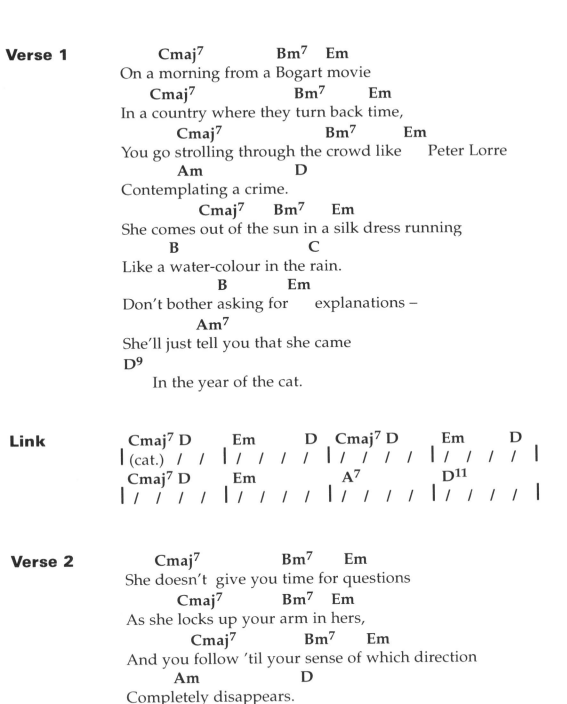

Cmaj^7 D | Em D | Cmaj^7 D | Em D
| (cat.) / / | / / / / | / / / / | / / / / |
Cmaj^7 D | Em | A^7 | D^{11}
| / / / / | / / / / | / / / / | / / / / |

Verse 2

Cmaj^7 Bm^7 Em
She doesn't give you time for questions
Cmaj^7 Bm^7 Em
As she locks up your arm in hers,
Cmaj^7 Bm^7 Em
And you follow 'til your sense of which direction
Am D
Completely disappears.

Cmaj^7 Bm^7 Em
By the blue-tiled walls near the market stalls
B C
There's a hidden door she leads you to:
B Em
"These days," she says, "I feel my life
Am^7
Just like a river running through
D^9
The year of the cat."

Link 2

Cmaj^7 D | Em D | Cmaj^7 D | Em D
| (cat.) / / | / / / / | / / / / | / / / / |
Cmaj^7 D | Em | A^7 | D^{11}
| / / / / | / / / / | / / / / | / / / / |

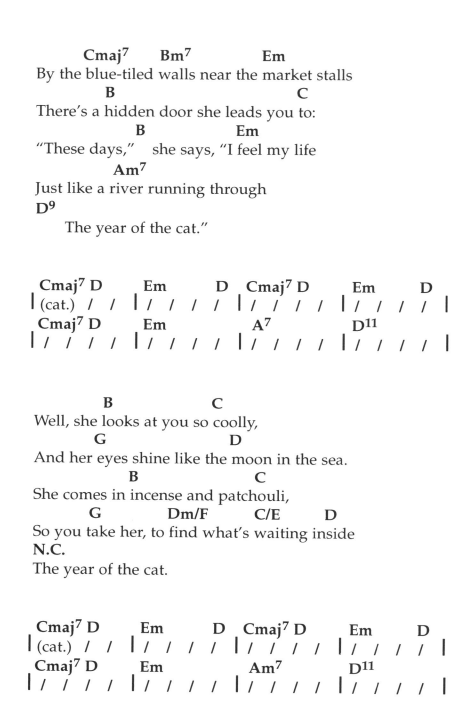

Bridge

B C
Well, she looks at you so coolly,
G D
And her eyes shine like the moon in the sea.
B C
She comes in incense and patchouli,
G Dm/F C/E D
So you take her, to find what's waiting inside
N.C.
The year of the cat.

Link 3

Cmaj^7 D | Em D | Cmaj^7 D | Em D
| (cat.) / / | / / / / | / / / / | / / / / |
Cmaj^7 D | Em | Am^7 | D^{11}
| / / / / | / / / / | / / / / | / / / / |

Acoustic Guitar solo

Cmaj7 D   Em   x3 Am7   D9

‖: / / / / | / / / / :‖ / / / / | / / / / |

Gmaj7   Cmaj7   Gmaj7   Cmaj7

| / / / / | / / / / | / / / / | / / / / |

Emaj7   Am   D

| / / / / | / / / / | / / / / | / / / / |

Electric Guitar solo

D   Gmaj7   D   Gmaj7

| / / / / | / / / / | / / / / | / / / / |

Bm   B/D♯   C/E   A/C♯

| / / / / | / / / / | / / / / | / / / / | / / / / |

Saxophone solo

Cmaj7 D   Em   D Cmaj7 D   Em   D

| / / / / | / / / / | / / / / | / / / / |

Cmaj7 D   Em   Am7   D9

| / / / / | / / / / | / / / / | / / / / |

Verse 3

     Cmaj7   Bm7   Em
One morning comes and you're still with her,
     Cmaj7   Bm7   Em
And the bus and the tourists are gone,
      Cmaj7   Bm7   Em
And you've thrown away your   choice and lost your ticket
    Am   D
So you have to stay on.
      Cmaj7   Bm7   Em
But the drum-beat strains of the night remain
    B   C
In the rhythm of the new-born day,
         B   Em
You know sometime   you're bound to leave her
     Am7
But for now you're going to stay
D9
    In the year of the cat.

Coda

| | Cmaj⁷ D | Em | D | Cmaj⁷ D | Em | D |

‖: (cat.) / / | / / / / | / / / / | / / / / |

Cmaj⁷ D   Em   Am⁷   D⁹

| / / / / | / / / / | / / / / | / / / / :‖

Hmmn, year of the

Saxophone solo 2

Gmaj⁷   Cmaj⁷   Gmaj⁷   Cmaj⁷

| / / / / | / / / / | / / / / | / / / / |

Emaj⁷   Am   D

| / / / / | / / / / | / / / / | / / / / |

Cmaj⁷ D   Em   D   Cmaj⁷ D   Em   D

‖: / / / / | / / / / | / / / / | / / / / |

Cmaj⁷ D   Em   Am⁷   D⁹

| / / / / | / / / / | / / / / | / / / / :‖

Cmaj⁷ D   Em   D

‖: / / / / | / / / / :‖ *(fade)*

You've Got A Friend

**Words and Music by
CAROLE KING**

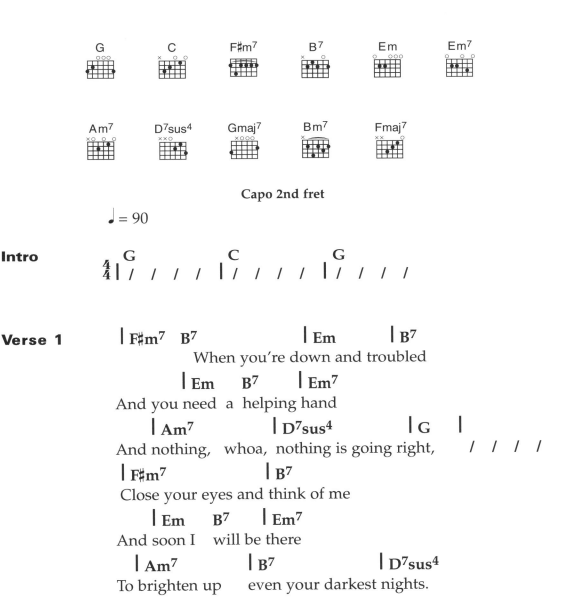

Capo 2nd fret

♩ = 90

Intro

$\frac{4}{4}$ | G / / / / | C / / / / | G / / / |

Verse 1

| F♯m⁷ B⁷ | Em | B⁷
　　　　When you're down and troubled
　　| Em   B⁷ | Em⁷
And you need a helping hand
　　| Am⁷ | D⁷sus⁴ | G |
And nothing,   whoa, nothing is going right,　　/ / / /
| F♯m⁷ | B⁷
　Close your eyes and think of me
　　| Em   B⁷ | Em⁷
And soon I   will be there
　　| Am⁷ | B⁷ | D⁷sus⁴
To brighten up   even your darkest nights.

Chorus 1

| | |G |Gmaj7 |C |Am7

You just call out my name, and you know wherever I am

|D7sus4 |G |Gmaj7 |D7sus4 |

I'll come running, oh yeah baby, to see you again. / / / /

|G |Gmaj7 |C |Em

Winter, spring, summer, or fall, all you got to do is call

|C Bm7 |D7sus4

And I'll be there, yeah, yeah, yeah.

|G

You've got a friend.

Link

C   G

| / / / / | / / / / |

Verse 2

|F#m7 B7 |Em |B7 |Em

If the sky__ above you should turn dark

B7 |Em7

And full of clouds

|Am7 |D7sus4 |G |

And that old north wind should begin to blow,___ / / / /

|F#m7 |B7 |Em B7 |Em7

Keep your head together and call my name out loud

|Am7 |B7 |D7sus4

Soon I'll be knocking upon your door.

Chorus 2

| | |G |Gmaj7 |C |Am7

You just call out my name and you know wherever I am

|D7sus4 |G | |D7sus4 |

I'll come running, oh yes I will, to see you again.

|G |Gmaj7 |C |Em

Winter, spring, summer or fall, all you got to do is call

|C Bm7 |D7sus4

And I'll be there, yeah, yeah, yeah.

Bridge

　　　　　　| Fmaj7　　　　　　　| C
Hey, ain't it good to know that you've got a friend
　　　　| G　　　　　　| Gmaj7
When people can be so cold ?
　　　　　　| C　　　　　| Fmaj7
They'll hurt you and desert you,
　　　　　　　| Em7　　　　　　　| A7
Well they'll take your soul if you let them.
　　　　　　　　| D7sus4
Oh yeah, but don't you let them.

Chorus 3

　　| 　　　　　　| G　　| Gmaj7　　　　| C　　　　　　| Am7
　　　You just call out my name and you know wherever I am
| D7sus4　　| G　　　　|　　　　　　　| D7sus4
　I'll come running　　　　to see you again.
　　　|
Oh babe, don't you know that,
| G　　　　　　　　| Gmaj7
Winter spring summer or fall, hey now,
| C　　　　　　　　　| Em
All you've got to do is call.____
　　　　　| C　　　| Bm7
Lord, I'll be there, yes I will.
| D7sus4　　　　　| G
　　You've got a friend.

Coda

| C　　　　　　| G
　You've got a friend –
| C　　　　　　　　　　| G
　Ain't it good to know you've got a friend,
　　| C　　　　　　| G
Ain't it good to know you've got a friend,
　| C　　　　　| Gsus4　G　‖
Oh yeah, yeah, you've got a friend.

You Wear It Well

Words and Music by
ROD STEWART AND MARTIN QUITTENTON

D   Em   F#m   G   A   A⁷sus⁴

♩ = 126 (half feel time)

Intro

$\frac{6}{4}$ | D / / / / / / $\frac{4}{4}$ | Em / / / / | / / / / |

$\frac{6}{4}$ | Em F#m G / / / / $\frac{4}{4}$ | A / / / / | / / / / |

$\frac{6}{4}$ | D / / / / / / $\frac{4}{4}$ | Em / / / / | / / / / |

$\frac{6}{4}$ | Em F#m G / / / / $\frac{4}{4}$ | A / / / / ‖

(a tempo)

Verse 1

      A   D   G
      I had nothing to do on this hot afternoon
          A   D
But to settle down and write you a line;
           G
I've been meaning to phone you but from Minnesota –
A   D
Hell, it's been a very long time:
          A
You wear it well,
    Em   F#m   G   A
A little old-fashioned but that's all right.

Verse 2

```
        D          G
Well, I suppose you're thinking, "I bet he's sinking
        A                          D
Or he wouldn't get in touch with me."
          G
Though I ain't begging or losing my head,
   A              D
I sure do want you to know
                    A
That you wear it well,
Em          F♯m       G       A
There ain't a lady in the land so fine, oh my.
```

Verse 3

```
        D              G
Remember them basement parties, your brother's karate,
      A                  D
The all-day rock and roll shows.
          G
Them homesick blues and the radical views
A                     D
Haven't left a mark on you:
              A
You wear it well,
   Em         F♯m     G        A
A little out of time but I don't mind.
```

Bridge

```
          D     G                      D
But I ain't forgetting that you were once mine
          G                 D
But I blew it without even trying.
                  G
Now I'm eating my heart out
A                       D
Trying to get a letter through.
```

Violin solo

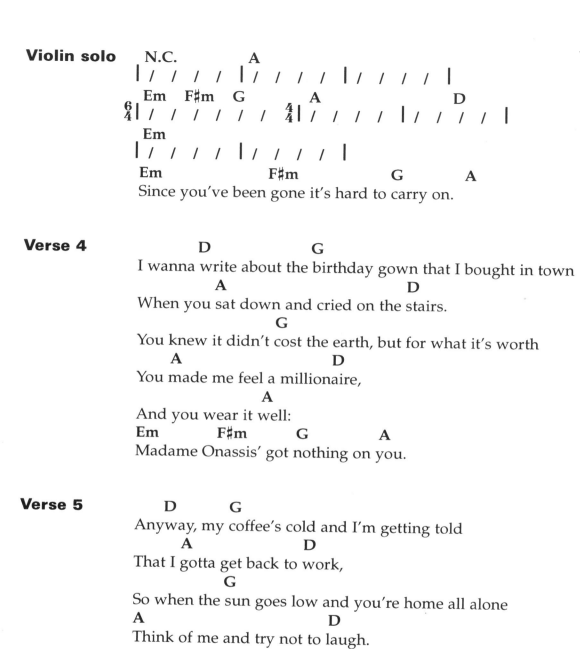

N.C.   A

| / / / / | / / / / | / / / / |

Em F♯m G   A   D

6/4 | / / / / / / 4/4 | / / / / | / / / / |

Em

| / / / / | / / / / |

Em   F♯m   G   A

Since you've been gone it's hard to carry on.

Verse 4

         D   G

I wanna write about the birthday gown that I bought in town

          A   D

When you sat down and cried on the stairs.

             G

You knew it didn't cost the earth, but for what it's worth

     A   D

You made me feel a millionaire,

         A

And you wear it well:

Em   F♯m   G   A

Madame Onassis' got nothing on you.

Verse 5

     D   G

Anyway, my coffee's cold and I'm getting told

       A   D

That I gotta get back to work,

        G

So when the sun goes low and you're home all alone

A   D

Think of me and try not to laugh.

       A

And I wear it well,

Em   F♯m   G   A

I don't object if you call-collect.

                  D   G   D
'Cause I ain't forgetting that you were once mine
            G   D
But I blew it without even trying,
            G
Now I'm eating my heart out
A^7sus^4
Trying to get back to you.

Coda

D   Em
$\frac{6}{4}$ | / / / / / / $\frac{4}{4}$ | / / / / | / / / / |

Em   F#m   G   A
$\frac{6}{4}$ | / / / / / / $\frac{4}{4}$ | / / / / | / / / / |

D
$\frac{6}{4}$ | / / / / / / |

Em
     I love you, I love you, I love you, I love you, I love you.

Em   F#m   G   A
$\frac{6}{4}$ | / / / / / / $\frac{4}{4}$ | / / / / | / / / / |

D   Em
$\frac{6}{4}$ | / / / / / / $\frac{4}{4}$ | / / / / | / / / / |

Em   F#m   G   A
$\frac{6}{4}$ | / / / / / / $\frac{4}{4}$ | / / / / | / / / / |

D   Em
After all the years I hope it's the same address. | / / / / |

Em   F#m   G   A
$\frac{6}{4}$ | / / / / / / $\frac{4}{4}$ | / / / / | / / / / |

D   Em
Since you've been gone it's hard to carry on.

Em   F#m   G   A
$\frac{6}{4}$ | / / / / / / $\frac{4}{4}$ | / / / / | / / / / | *(fade)* ‖

Songs guitars were meant to play

Essential Acoustic Playlist 2
9854A   VC   ISBN: 1-84328-411-1

A Minha Meninha (The Bees) – Ain't That Enough (Teenage Fanclub) – All Together Now (The Farm) – Alright (Supergrass) – Am I Wrong (Mull Historical Society) – American English (Idlewild) – Average Man (Turin Brakes) – Beetlebum (Blur) – Breakfast at Tiffany's (Deep Blue Something) – Buy It In Bottles (Richard Ashcroft) – Can You Dig It? (The Mock Turtles) – Caught By The River (Doves) – Coffee & TV (Blur) – Come Away With Me (Norah Jones) – Come Back To What You Know (Embrace) – Common People (Pulp) – Crazy Beat (Blur) – Creep (Radiohead) – A Design For Life (Manic Street Preachers) – Distant Sun (Crowded House) – Don't Let Me Down Gently (The Wonderstuff) – Don't Think You're The First (The Coral) – Everlong (Foo Fighters) – Fallen Angel (Elbow) – Fastboy (The Bluetones) – The Final Arrears (Mull Historical Society) – Forget About Tomorrow (Feeder) – Getting Away With It (Electronic) – Go To Sleep (Radiohead) – Grace (Supergrass) – Here's Where The Story Ends (The Sundays) – High And Dry (Radiohead) – History (The Verve) – Hooligan (Embrace) – I Need Direction (Teenage Fanclub) – I Will (Radiohead) – (I'm Gonna) Cry Myself Blind (Primal Scream) – In A Room (Dodgy) – It's True That We Love One Another (The White Stripes) – Just When You're Thinkin' Things Over (The Charlatans) – La Breeze (Simian) – Lilac Wine (Jeff Buckley) – A Little Like You (Grand Drive) – Live In A Hiding Place (Idlewild) – Lucky (Radiohead) – A Man Needs To Be Told (The Charlatans) – No Surprises (Radiohead) – Only Happy When It Rains (Garbage) – Out Of Time (Blur) – Painkiller (Turin Brakes) – Pass It On (The Coral) – Personal Jesus (Johnny Cash) – Pineapple Head (Crowded House) – Poor Misguided Fool (Starsailor) – Road Rage (Catatonia) – Seen The Light (Supergrass) – Seven Nation Army (The White Stripes) – Shine On (The House Of Love) – Silence Is Easy (Starsailor) – Sk8ter Boi (Avril Lavigne) – Stay Away From Me (The Star Spangles) – There There (Radiohead) – Thinking About Tomorrow (Beth Orton) – This Is How It Feels (Inspiral Carpets) – Wake Up Boo! (The Boo Radleys) – Words (Doves) – Yoshimi Battles The Pink Robots (Flaming Lips) – You're So Pretty – We're So Pretty (The Charlatans) – You've Got Her In Your Pocket (The White Stripes)

Essential Acoustic Playlist
9701A   VC   ISBN: 1-84328-207-0

All The Small Things (Blink 182) – All You Good Good People (Embrace) – Angie (The Rolling Stones) – Any Day Now (Elbow) – Bittersweet Symphony (The Verve) – Buddy (Lemonheads) – Burning Down The House (Talking Heads) – Central Reservation (Beth Orton) – Come Together (Primal Scream) – Cryin' (Aerosmith) – Don't Dream It's Over (Crowded House) – The Drugs Don't Work (The Verve) – Empty At The End (Electric Soft Parade) – Everybody Hurts (R.E.M.) – Everyday Is Like Sunday (Morrissey) – Fast Car (Tracey Chapman) – Fat Lip (Sum 41) – Fell In Love With A Girl (The White Stripes) – Fireworks (Embrace) – Fly Away (Lenny Kravitz) – Future Boy (Turin Brakes) – Going Places (Teenage Fanclub) – Good Riddance (Green Day) – Heaven Knows I'm Miserable Now (The Smiths) – Hotel California (The Eagles) – Hotel Yorba (The White Stripes) – Hunter (Dido) – It's A Shame About Ray (Lemonheads) – Karma Police (Radiohead) – Kiss Me (Sixpence None The Richer) – Losing My Religion (R.E.M.) – Love Burns (Black Rebel Motorcycle Club) – The Man Who Told Everything (Doves) – Mansize Rooster (Supergrass) – Mellow Doubt (Teenage Fanclub) – Movin' On Up (Primal Scream) – Moving (Supergrass) – Mr. Jones (Counting Crows) – Next Year (Foo Fighters) – Novocaine For The Soul (Eels) – Over The Rainbow (Eva Cassidy) – Panic (The Smiths) – Porcelain (Moby) – Pounding (Doves) – Powder Blue (Elbow) – Rhythm & Blues Alibi (Gomez) – Save Tonight (Eagle Eye Cherry) – Silent Sigh (Badly Drawn Boy) – Secret Smile (Semisonic) – Shot Shot (Gomez) – Silent To The Dark (Electric Soft Parade) – Slight Return (The Bluetones) – Soak Up The Sun (Sheryl Crow) – Something In My Eye (Ed Harcourt) – Something To Talk About (Badly Drawn Boy) – Song 2 (Blur) – Song For The Lovers (Richard Ashcroft) – Standing Still (Jewel) – Street Spirit (Fade Out) (Radiohead) – Teenage Dirtbag (Wheatus) – Tender (Blur) – There Goes The Fear (Doves) – Time In A Bottle (Jim Croce) – Underdog (Save Me) (Turin Brakes) – Walking After You (Foo Fighters) – Warning (Green Day) – Waterloo Sunset (The Kinks) – Weather With You (Crowded House) – Wicked Game (Chris Isaak) – Wild Wood (Paul Weller)

Classic Acoustic Playlist
9806A   VC   ISBN: 1-84328-332-8

Ain't No Sunshine (Bill Withers) – All Tomorrow's Parties (The Velvet Underground) – Alone Again Or (Love) – Another Brick In The Wall Part II (Pink Floyd) – Bad Moon Rising (Creedence Clearwater Revival) – Black Magic Woman (Fleetwood Mac) – Both Sides Now (Joni Mitchell) – Brain Damage/Eclipse (Pink Floyd) – Break On Through (The Doors) – California Dreamin' (The Mamas & The Papas) – Cocaine (Eric Clapton) – Cosmic Dancer (T. Rex) – Crazy Little Thing Called Love (Queen) – Daydream Believer (The Monkees) – Days (The Kinks) – Desperado (The Eagles) – Eight Miles High (The Byrds) – Everybody's Talkin' (Harry Nilsson) – Five Years (David Bowie) – For What It's Worth (Buffalo Springfield) – Fortunate Son (Creedence Clearwater Revival) – Get It On (T. Rex) – Handbags & Gladrags (Rod Stewart) – Happy (The Rolling Stones) – He Ain't Heavy, He's My Brother (The Hollies) – Heroin (The Velvet Underground) – A Horse With No Name (America) – I Feel The Earth Move (Carole King) – It's Only Rock And Roll (The Rolling Stones) – It's Too Late (Carole King) – Itchycoo Park (The Small Faces) – Layla (Eric Clapton) – Leaving On A Jet Plane (John Denver) – Life On Mars (David Bowie) – Light My Fire (The Doors) – London Calling (The Clash) – Long Time Gone (Crosby, Stills & Nash) – Long Train Runnin' (The Doobie Brothers) – The Look Of Love (Dusty Springfield) – Lust For Life (Iggy Pop) – Maggie May (Rod Stewart) – Make Me Smile (Come Up And See Me) (Steve Harley & Cockney Rebel) – Miss You (The Rolling Stones) – Moondance (Van Morrison) – More Than A Feeling (Boston) – Mustang Sally (Wilson Pickett) – New Kid In Town (The Eagles) – Oliver's Army (Elvis Costello) – Pale Blue Eyes (The Velvet Underground) – Perfect Day (Lou Reed) – Silence Is Golden (The Tremeloes) – Sloop John B (The Beach Boys) – Smoke On The Water (Deep Purple) – Space Oddity (David Bowie) – Start Me Up (The Rolling Stones) – Strange Kind Of Woman (Deep Purple) – Stuck In The Middle With You (Stealers Wheel) – Summer In The City (Lovin' Spoonful) – Sunny Afternoon (The Kinks) – Suzanne (Leonard Cohen) – Sweet Home Alabama (Lynyrd Skynyrd) – Tempted (The Squeeze) – Tequila Sunrise (The Eagles) – Turn Turn Turn (The Byrds) – Venus In Furs (The Velvet Underground) – We Gotta Get Out Of This Place (The Animals) – Whiter Shade Of Pale (Procol Harum) – Wuthering Heights (Kate Bush) – You're My Best Friend (Queen) - You've Got A Friend (James Taylor)

Essential Acoustic Strumalong
9808A   BK/CD   ISBN: 1-84328-335-2

All You Good Good People (Embrace) - American English (Idlewild) - The Drugs Don't Work (The Verve) - Grace (Supergrass) – Handbags And Gladrags (Stereophonics) - Hotel Yorba (The White Stripes) - Karma Police (Radiohead) - Love Burns (Black Rebel Motorcycle Club) - Poor Misguided Fool (Starsailor) - Powder Blue (Elbow) - Silent Sigh (Badly Drawn Boy) - Silent To The Dark (The Electric Soft Parade) - Tender (Blur) - There Goes The Fear (Doves) - Underdog (Save Me) (Turin Brakes)

Classic Acoustic Strumalong
9844A   BK/CD   ISBN: 1-84328-397-2

Alone Again Or (Love) – Another Brick In The Wall Part II (Pink Floyd) – Cocaine (Eric Clapton) – Get It On (T. Rex) – Handbags And Gladrags (Rod Stewart) – London Calling (The Clash) – Lust For Life (Iggy Pop) – Make Me Smile (Come Up And See Me) (Steve Harley & Cockney Rebel) – Mustang Sally (Wilson Pickett) – Perfect Day (Lou Reed) – Start Me Up (The Rolling Stones) – Stuck In The Middle With You (Stealers Wheel) – Sunny Afternoon (The Kinks) – Venus In Furs (Velvet Underground) – Whiter Shade Of Pale (Procol Harum)

Available now in all good music shops